# From Stuttering to Fluency:

# Manage Your Emotions and Live More Fully

Gunars K. Neiders, Psy.D. Ph.D.

With

Will Ross

ISBN: 1494302586
ISBN-13: 978-1494302580

DEDICATION


To Regine and Cindy
And
To Albert Ellis

# CONTENTS

# 1 GET READY FOR CHANGE

**In this chapter you will:**

- Learn what this book has to offer you and why it's different from other books about stuttering.

- Get to know many famous people who stutter.

## What is stuttering?

Does that sound like a silly question? Surely everybody knows what stuttering is.

Random House dictionary defines stuttering as

> "to speak in such a way that the rhythm is interrupted by repetitions, blocks or spasms, or prolongations of sounds or syllables, sometimes accompanied by contortions of the face and body."

To most people, this definition of stuttering is more than adequate. It's probably what most people mean when they talk or think about stuttering.

In this book, we will show that contrary to popular opinion, the standard definition of stuttering is not

1

adequate. We'll show you a new, more complete way to think about the subject. You'll see how our model shows that there is more to stuttering than interrupted speech and "contortions of the face and body."

You will also learn why so many stuttering therapies fail. But for now, here's a hint: most therapies fail because they begin with an inadequate, incomplete understanding of what stuttering is.

Our aim is to provide a new understanding of stuttering that will revolutionize the way you think about it. You'll develop a deeper understanding of its causes and its effects.

And along with this deeper understanding, you'll learn how our expanded model of stuttering provides a clue as to what effective therapy might entail. Better yet, we'll show you how you can teach yourself an effective therapy aimed at the entire stuttering experience.

## Who Stutters?

The history books, not to mention the gossip pages of newspapers and supermarket tabloids, are full of the names of famous people who have or who currently stutter: Moses, hero of the Old Testament; Battus who founded the Greek colony at Cyrene in Libya (630 BCE); the Roman emperor Claudius (41-54 CE); the Byzantine emperor Michael II the Stutterer (820-829 CE); the French king Louis II (877-879); the English kings Charles I (1629-1649) and George IV (1937-1952); and Britain's prime minister Winston Churchill; the philosopher Aristotle; Charles Darwin; Tiger Woods; Mel Tillis; James Earl Jones; Marilyn Monroe; Prince Albert of Monaco; and business leaders Jack Welch and John Sculley.

A list of all the famous — and infamous — stutterers in history would be too long for this book. We don't know the name of everyone who stutters because they are not all famous. What we do know is that there are many people all over the world who stutter. How many? One estimate suggests that approximately 1% of the world's population stutters. That's about 66 million stutterers in the world! More than 3 million of them live in the United States.

## What to expect

If you're one of those 66 million people who stutter, then this book is for you. We hope it will also interest your friends, family, teachers, coworkers, employers, and speech therapists.

Here are some of the things you'll discover.

In the next chapter, you'll learn about traditional treatments for stuttering; you'll learn about their strengths and weaknesses, their successes and failures. Chapter 3 tells how I (G.N.) tried 17 different therapies to overcome my stuttering before I finally overcame it with the methods you'll learn in this book. In Chapter 4, we'll give you our expanded definition of stuttering and explain how this new definition benefits you in ways you never thought possible. If you've ever wondered why you stutter, Chapter 5 gives you the answer. In Chapter 6, you'll learn how you can use the expanded definition of stuttering, coupled with a deeper understanding of its causes, to create a tailor-made treatment plan for yourself that supplements the work you do with your speech therapist, if you have one. In Chapter 7, you'll learn how to put your treatment plan to work so you get maximum benefit from it. In Chapter 8, you'll discover a new way of looking at yourself that will free you from self-doubt, shame, and embarrassment. Chapter 9 will teach you ways to directly control your speech. Chapter 10 will reinforce all you've learned and look ahead to what you can expect in the future. Finally, we've added Appendices that provide additional methods you can use to hold your head up high and speak with confidence.

**Remember this:**

- Most stuttering therapies fail because they begin with an inadequate, incomplete definition of stuttering.

- Many people who stutter lead full and interesting lives and don't allow their stuttering to hold them back. You can do it too!

# 2 THE SEARCH FOR A CURE

In this chapter you will:

- Discover some of the bizarre historical methods as well as some modern methods used to treat stuttering.

- Learn about the strengths and weaknesses of modern stuttering treatments.

With over 66 million stutterers worldwide, and many more in recorded and unrecorded history, it's no wonder that a multitude of treatments have been tried. A number of the methods used in the pre-scientific era were quite bizarre, and a few seem outright barbaric.

As far as we know, Moses was never cured of his stuttering but the Greek orator Demosthenes (383-322 BCE) apparently had some success with a treatment suggested by the actor Satyrus. The thespian encouraged Demosthenes to talk with pebbles in his mouth, look in the mirror as he talked, and recite poetry while walking uphill.

The Byzantine physician and medical writer, Aetius of Amida, whose works date back to the 6th century, advocated the first known surgical cure for stuttering. He believed that surgically separating the frenum, a small fold of tissue on the underside of the tongue, would cure stuttering.

Thereafter, surgery became a popular method for curing stuttering and remained fashionable for several centuries. Johann Frederick Dieffenbach (1795-1847) a German surgeon and H. de Chegoin, in Paris, both devised their own special surgical procedures to cure stuttering. But the records show that neither of these gentleman had any real success with their methods.

In 1817, J.M.G. Itard reported that a special gold or ivory fork placed under the tongue had cured stuttering in two cases. His boasts of success were short-lived as reports from different sources revealed that the cure had not been permanent.

Charles Canon Kingsley (1819-1875), an orator who stuttered until the age of 40, proposed that a combination of dumbbell exercises and placing a piece of cork between the back teeth would cure stuttering.

Over the past two hundred years, a variety of other treatments have been tried. Most have failed to provide consistently positive results. Some of these methods include: direct suggestion, hypnosis, speech drills, distraction, and relaxation. Therapies that control the rhythm and timing of speech have also been tried.

Some speech therapists have experimented with mechanical methods to cure stuttering. The United States Patent Office has approximately seventy prosthetic devices on its register. These devices are inserted into the mouth or over the Adam's apple so that they change the way you breathe.

Other therapists have taken a "carrot and stick" approach. They praise their clients for fluent speech and punish them whenever they stutter. Some have even administered an electrical shock to their clients as a punishment for stuttering.

Other therapists have experimented with a more humane method of treatment: drowning out, or masking, noises in the room. Others have tried Delayed Auditory Feedback, a method in which the stutterer's voice is recorded and then played back into his or her ear a few milliseconds later.

Despite their unusual nature and their inconsistent results, many of these techniques are still used today in either their original form or with slight modifications. The quest to find a consistently effective cure for stuttering will no doubt result in more strange methods being proposed in the future.

Fortunately, not all treatment methods used today are as weird as the "cures" that have been tried in the past.

Modern stuttering therapy is practiced by Speech Language Professionals (SLPs) who are well educated with degrees specializing in speech therapy. Their education is broad –based, covering all communication problems including articulation disorders and fluency disorders. SLPs are licensed by the state in which they practice.

Current stuttering therapy, as practiced by most SLPs, focuses on retraining the muscle groups that are used in producing and regulating breath, the voice- and sound-producing muscles (the vocal folds), and the speech-shaping muscles such as the lips and tongue. The two main therapies used today are known as fluency shaping and stuttering modification. Some SLPs use one or the other; many use integrative therapies that combine the two.

Let's take a closer look at fluency shaping and stuttering modification.

## Fluency Shaping

Most people who stutter would like to have totally fluent speech, without blocks or repetitions. That is the ultimate goal of fluency shaping.

Speech Language Professionals who specialize in fluency shaping will teach you to master certain motor skills and/or muscular skills. These are the skills that are required for normal speech. The aim is to move your muscles in a particular pattern. These patterns are called *target behaviors* and are taught in sequence. Mastering these target behaviors to achieve completely fluent speech takes a tremendous amount of practice. To make it easier for you to master these skills, your SLP will break them down into a series of steps.

The first step is to prolong your speech and to notice how your muscles are moving. Sometimes, you'll have the assistance of a computer to give you feedback; if a computer isn't available, you'll receive feedback from your SLP. The aim is to practice until your muscles move in the same way as a speaker without a stutter. You'll start by making sounds, then syllables, then words, then simple sentences, and ultimately conversational speech.

Next, you'll learn to use "easy onsets" where you make sure that your tongue and lips do not touch each other or the roof of your mouth. Again, you'll often have the aid of feedback from a computer or your SLP. Once you're able to easily make the sound and maintain it, while holding your mouth, tongue, and lips in the correct position, you'll progress on to syllables, words, sentences, and speech.

Finally, when you're able to carry out normal conversation, without the aid of a computer or your SLP's guidance, you'll practice using these techniques in the real-world, outside your SLP's office.

This final step can be challenging and not always successful; you may find it daunting and feel overwhelmed by it. If that's the case, you can practice your new skills with graduate and undergraduate students, your SLP's secretary and other staff members, or other places where you feel safe before taking your skills out into the big wide world.

You can also add the methods you'll learn in this book to boost your confidence so that you're not overwhelmed by anxiety each time you practice your new skills in public.

## Stuttering Modification

If your SLP specializes in stuttering modification, you'll learn to modify your speech so that it is continually moving forward even though you continue to stutter. Another goal of stuttering modification is for you to learn to speak with minimal abnormality.

Stuttering modification SLPs are guided by the acronym MIDVAS, which stands for Motivation, Identification, Desensitization, Variation, Approximation and Stabilization.

To motivate you, your SLP will build your desire to do the essential practice to meet your speech goals.

Next, you and your SLP will identify the obvious and not-so-obvious things you do when you stutter.

Having identified what you do when you stutter, your SLP will encourage you to get used to those behaviors so that you're no longer bothered by them. For example, you may be encouraged to stutter more than you normally do.

Your SLP will have you vary the way you talk. For example, he or she may have you repeat words that you stumble on in a way that is imperfect, but different from your usual speech. Or you may be asked to stop speaking midway through a word, and to hold onto the stuttering moment until you're confident you can complete the word in a slow, purposeful, prolonged way.

The final exercise is to practice talking using the same posture that a non-stutterer would employ to say a particular sound or word. You'll be asked to monitor your speech and may go on "field trips" with your SLP to reinforce your gains.

Once you've mastered these steps, you'll continue practicing them to over-learn them until they feel natural to you and you can use them in your normal day-to-day activities.

## Strengths and weaknesses

Whether your SLP specializes in fluency shaping or stuttering modification, you will probably see him or her once or twice a week. You may even enroll in an intensive course lasting two to three weeks for nine hours per day. There are many ways that either treatment can be modified and adapted to suit your needs.

SLPs from the fluency shaping school assume that you stutter because that's the way you learned to talk. They consider stutter-free speech as the only successful outcome. They won't try to reduce your fears and anxieties about stuttering but believe they will naturally disappear once you speak without stuttering.

On the other hand, SLPs from the stuttering modification school will encourage you to confront your fears by deliberately stuttering and remaining in situations you find difficult.

Long-term studies indicate that for most people, neither of these treatments results in lasting, stutter-free speech. However, stutterers who have learned to change their attitude towards stuttering and overcome their fear of speaking have a better outcome than those who do not adjust their attitude. As you'll learn in later chapters, we believe changing your attitude towards yourself, others, and life in general will significantly enhance the effectiveness of therapy. In fact, for many people who stutter, a change in attitude is all they need to speak more fluently.

## Mechanical speech aids

Recent advances in technology and miniaturization have led to the development of a device similar to a hearing aid. The device has a microphone and an earplug. When you speak, the microphone records your speech and plays it back to you through the earplug. The device delays your speech by 50 to 250 milliseconds and plays it back at a higher or lower pitch.

At the time of writing, there have been no long-term, scientific studies to determine how well these devices work or on what their effect may be on the brain development of children.

And so the search for a universal, effective cure for stuttering goes on. In the next chapter, you'll learn how I (G.N.) tried 17 different therapies to overcome my stuttering before I finally overcame it with the methods you'll learn in this book.

## Remember this:

- Fluency shaping and stuttering modification are the two most commonly used methods of treating stuttering.

- Long-term studies indicate that for most people, neither of these treatments results in lasting, stutter-free speech.

- Stutterers who have learned to change their attitude

towards stuttering and overcome their fear of speaking have a better outcome than those who do not adjust their attitude.

# 3 HOPES AND DREAMS

**In this chapter you will:**

- Learn how one of the authors of this book tried 17 different therapies before conquering his stuttering.

- Get to know about a systematic, theory-based method to change your stuttering-related thoughts, feelings, and behaviors.

My co-author (W.R.) has never stuttered but I (G.N.) have stuttered to varying degrees throughout my life.

I was born in Latvia at a time when that country was independent. But Latvia's independence was shattered by a Soviet invasion that was soon followed by a Nazi invasion. My family and I lived in constant fear.

To my knowledge, no one in my family has ever stuttered, but within a few months of learning to talk, I began stuttering. I struggled with my words, and as I became more aware of my struggles, I felt helpless and hopeless. I began to doubt that I would ever be able to communicate effectively.

By the time I started school, my stuttering was so severe

that I refused to talk. For example, on one occasion when I needed to go to the bathroom, I was so afraid to talk that I would not raise my hand and ask for permission to be excused. Instead, I tried to "hold it in." Much to my chagrin, my valiant attempt to hold it in failed with embarrassing results. I can still recall the small rivulet snaking its way toward the front of the room in the rows between the desks.

With the passage of time, I can now look back on that incident with amusement. I cannot say the same about another stuttering incident that occurred when I was twelve.

## A family's dream threatened

World War II had ended. Like many others from Eastern Europe, my family and I were living in a refugee camp, barely surviving on a subsistence diet: three daily meals of "slop". What we couldn't eat with the single spoon my family shared, we ate with our fingers. In an atmosphere reminiscent of a Charles Dickens novel, there were no second helpings.

We had one change of outer clothing, two sets of underwear and no entertainment except communal singing and soccer, played with a ball made of rags.

Although our schools in the camp had no books, we had excellent teachers. I was taught math by engineers, biology by doctors and nurses, and language by authors and poets. We each had a small slate tablet to write on, although once in a while we'd have paper and pencils or crayons which were a gift from American churches.

Life was bleak. However, we were not starving as we had been during our flight from the advancing Russian armies. Our girls and women were usually not attacked by the occupying United States soldiers. Many of the girls and women who had remained in Latvia under Russian occupation were not so lucky.

The situation in Latvia made returning to our homeland out of the question. My family's greatest wish was to immigrate to the United States. Because my father was a doctor and my mother a dentist, the United States government was willing to accept us for resettlement, provided we could pass a series of health tests and demonstrate that we were not Nazi sympathizers.

The interview with my father, mother, and two older sisters went well. My youngest sister, then aged 2, just smiled. Then it came my turn. When the immigration officer asked me my name, I had one of my silent blocks. After 5 breaths, I still could not get a sound to come out of my mouth.

By that time I had already been exposed to some "stuttering therapy". The two or three self-proclaimed stuttering therapists had done nothing except teach me to keep trying to talk. When I was asked my name, I was determined to say "Gunars". But nothing came out. Nothing! I felt terrified that my secondary stuttering symptoms and non-response would reflect on my mental competence and place my family's immigration dream in jeopardy.

My mother and father told the US Consular representative that I stuttered. He must have understood. He kindly gave me a pencil and a piece of paper to write my name on. However, in my panic, and possibly due to what I'd learned in my stuttering therapy, I was determined to say my name. Writing my name would have been an admission of failure and unworthiness. I persevered, struggling to speak while exhibiting all types of secondary stuttering symptoms. Yet the ominous silence persisted.

Eventually we were escorted out of the office. My father

stayed behind for a while, and I fled into the woods, hiding out for 8 hours. Emerging from my hiding place, I wept and could not be consoled. I spent the next two or three weeks alone, blaming myself for letting my family down. I don't remember all the details of those days, but I recall it was traumatic.

Although school was in session during those weeks, I had no contact with my school mates or soccer buddies; I ate and slept only sporadically. I would not talk with my family. I knew I had swept away their dreams — not only because of my stuttering, but because of not responding when asked to write my name. I blamed myself mercilessly and would not allow anyone to console me.

Happily, we were eventually cleared for immigration to the United States. I can only assume that the kind US Consulate employee had been exposed to other people who stuttered and knew that I was not going to end up as a ward of the state.

Safely settled in the United States, I began the search for a cure for my struggling, incoherent speech. I tried seventeen different therapies. I began each new therapy with a wave of hope, only to have that hope dashed and be replaced by disappointment. This experience taught me that there are at least seventeen different stuttering therapies that don't work!

## Lifelong stuttering

My experiences looking for a cure for stuttering are typical for adults who stutter. Approximately 40% of children who stutter will overcome their problem without any professional help by the time they're seven years old. Another 40% will overcome the problem with the aid of a professional. The remaining 20% will develop chronic, lifelong stuttering.

FROM STUTTERING TO FLUENCY

Lifelong stutterers often find that not only do they have to deal with repetitions and blocks in their speech, but they also have unhealthy negative emotions, distressing thoughts, and unusual stuttering-related behaviors. These lifelong stutterers may speak fluently some of the time, but even with therapy, they're just as likely to relapse and return to stuttering and all the thoughts, feelings, and actions that go along with it.

Why is therapy so ineffective for lifelong stutterers?

We believe the low success rate is the result of SLPs focusing exclusively on changing the mechanics of speech. That is, they focus on what you do with your vocal folds, your mouth, your breathing, your lips, your tongue, etc. Few, if any, therapies focus on your thoughts, your feelings, or your behaviors. Those therapies that do address these aspects of stuttering do so in an unstructured, half-hearted, or haphazard way.

People who learn to control their anxiety about stuttering often report that they become more fluent. With or without additional fluency, less anxiety and greater participation in life adds to the overall quality of our existence. The real tragedy of SLPs not directly or systematically addressing the fears and anxieties of their clients is that many people who stutter are missing out on so much that life has to offer.

## It's not as bad as it seems

The good news is that there is a systematic, theory-based method to change your stuttering-related thoughts, feelings, and behaviors. The method is called Rational Emotive Behavior Therapy (REBT).

The vast majority of people who learn to use Rational Emotive Behavior Therapy in their lives do not stutter. They use REBT to overcome depression, anger, shame, and anxiety — the very same emotions that many people who stutter feel about their stuttering. They also use it to change some of their behaviors, such as avoiding talking to strangers or not applying for jobs they want — behaviors that are very familiar to many people who stutter.

Usually, people who use Rational Emotive Behavior Therapy learn to do so from a psychologist or from self-help books written by the creator of REBT, Dr. Albert Ellis. Unfortunately, few of the psychologists who teach REBT know anything about stuttering.

Although some SLPs will teach their clients how to use REBT, they usually do so only in passing and don't make it the primary focus of their therapy.

## Why are we so passionate about REBT?

You'll recall that I (G.N.) tried seventeen different therapies to cure my stuttering — none of which worked. My search for a cure eventually led me into the office of Albert Ellis, the creator of Rational Emotive Behavior Therapy. Dr. Ellis quickly convinced me that I could accept myself whether or not I stuttered; I did not need to speak fluently. Paradoxically, the moment I gave up the need to stop stuttering, I became much more fluent. In almost no time at all, Dr. Ellis was able to achieve what seventeen SLPs had failed to do: teach me to speak with imperfect fluency and to enjoy my life no matter how I speak!

If REBT can offer life-changing benefits to people who stutter, why is it that so few SLPs teach their clients to use it? We see two reasons for REBT's absence in the treatment of stuttering: (1) SLPs who know a lot about stuttering don't know much about REBT; and (2) psychologists who know a lot about REBT don't know much about stuttering. As a result, people who stutter and have the associated unhealthy feelings, thoughts, and actions that go along with stuttering are missing out on the benefits that an evidence-based therapy can deliver to them. What is missing from the treatment of stuttering is an approach that combines the best methods of addressing the mechanical, bodily aspects of stuttering with a proven method of addressing your stuttering-related thoughts, feelings, and actions.

Given present technology and what we know — and don't know — about stuttering, it's unlikely that an adult, lifelong stutterer can be cured of stuttering so that he or she always speaks fluently, and never again has the blocks or repetitions of the past.

The next best outcome — one that is well within the realms of possibility — is to speak fluently, or with minimal disfluency, for long periods of time. This outcome would also include rarely feeling any shame, anxiety, guilt, or other harmful emotions. It would allow people who stutter to enjoy a much greater participation in life without avoiding speaking opportunities.

There may not be a foolproof, guaranteed cure for stuttering. But take a moment to dream. Think how your life would be different if you did not stutter. How would you feel when talking to others, either in person or on the phone? Would you feel more relaxed in those situations than you do when you currently face those situations?

Imagine speaking without anxiety! How much more fluently do you think you would speak if you no longer felt anxious every time you opened your mouth? You may not be perfectly fluent, but almost certainly, you'd speak more fluently than you do presently.

What changes would you make if you didn't stutter? Now imagine making those lifestyle changes, regardless of whether or not you stutter.

When you learn Rational Emotive Behavior Therapy and

apply it consistently in your life, you can achieve the twin benefits of (1) speaking with less, or even no, anxiety; and (2) overcoming the tendency to avoid life-enhancing situations, such as applying for a better job or talking to attractive strangers.

Your SLP, if you have one, may know nothing about REBT. But by the time you've finished reading this book, you'll know enough to begin making these profound changes that REBT can bring.

But before we teach you how to use REBT, let's take a closer look at stuttering, what it is, and what causes it.

---

**Remember this:**

- Rational Emotive Behavior Therapy (REBT) is a systematic, theory-based method to change your stuttering-related thoughts, feelings, and behaviors.

- With REBT you can speak with little or no anxiety and overcome the tendency to avoid life-enhancing situations.

---

# 4 TOWARDS UNDERSTANDING

---

**In this chapter you will:**

- Learn a more complete definition of stuttering.

- Discover the role of thoughts, feelings, and actions in the stuttering experience.

---

## What is stuttering?

If you ask any of your friends who don't stutter to tell you what they think stuttering is, they'll probably tell you that it means that you have trouble saying some words. They'll tell you about repetitions and blocks and they may even mention that you move your head or blink your eyes whenever you talk.

To the outside observer, this is what it means to stutter. But for those of us who stutter, there is much more to it than what our friends can see and hear.

What your friends can't see is how you feel — how you feel before you speak, how you feel while you're speaking, and how you feel after you have finished speaking. What they can't see is what you think — what you think before you speak, what you think while you're speaking, and what you think after you have finished speaking. Your friends can't see all the planning you do — planning which words to use and which words to avoid. They can't see all the situations you avoid, such as turning down invitations to parties, not applying for jobs you want, or making sure that other family members answer the phone whenever it rings.

Most of your friends probably have no idea that stuttering has many faces and there are many aspects of lifelong stuttering that have absolutely nothing to do with speaking.

For too long, too many SLPs have — like your friends — focused almost exclusively on the mechanics of speech while not paying sufficient attention to these other aspects of stuttering: your thoughts, your feelings, and your actions. We believe that focusing on and overcoming many of these other, often overlooked, facets of stuttering is the key to coping with stuttering and to becoming more fluent.

So let's take another look at stuttering, and pay special attention to these other aspects. As we look at the multifaceted nature of lifelong stuttering, it's important to remember that not all of these aspects will apply to you. But many of them will be very familiar to you. Those aspects of stuttering that don't apply to you will be well known to other people who stutter.

## Seen and heard

The most obvious part of stuttering is the one your friends notice — you have trouble saying some words. Sometimes you repeat the first letter or first syllable of a word. At other times, you open your mouth to speak but no sounds emerge. Some of these speech difficulties occur before you even speak. As you plan what you are about to say and rehearse it in your mind, you are aware of repetitions and blocks.

Your speech, when it comes out, often does not have the same frequency as the speech of people who don't stutter. Your voice may be higher pitched or lower pitched. You may speak slower or faster than people who don't stutter. Sometimes you may speak in a singsong voice or emphasize words and syllables differently from the way people who don't stutter emphasize their words and syllables. Sometimes you may speak in a monotone without emphasizing any words or syllables. You may even speak as though you have a foreign accent.

Another aspect of stuttering for some people, and which is often, but not always, obvious to outside observers is unusual body movement. Many of the people you speak to won't notice that you avoid making eye contact with them, but they may notice that you blink your eyes whenever you speak. They may or may not notice that you snap your fingers, swing your hands, or swing your entire body back and forth. Some of your listeners will notice that you tense various muscles in your face, that your face twitches, and sometimes your head jerks when you speak. If they are very observant they may notice you tapping your right or left foot, or perhaps both of them. If you've had some types of speech therapy, you might have been taught to speak as though you are chewing at the same time so as to hide the fact that you have trouble saying some words. This simultaneous chewing and speaking may or may not be obvious to your listener.

Fortunately, even if you have body movements, most

people are not very observant, and unless your body movements are exaggerated, many of the people you speak to won't notice them. Even if they do notice some of the things you do when you speak, very few people will notice the things you avoid doing. People who stutter find many things to avoid, and chances are you're no different. Let's take a closer look at some of these avoidance behaviors that are common to people who stutter.

Perhaps you have difficulty with certain words or letters. You have probably decided that some sounds are difficult and that you will nearly always stutter when you try to say words that start with these sounds. To get around this problem, you'll try to avoid these words and substitute other words or phrases in their place. You'll find that you think ahead and plan multiple ways to avoid these difficult sounds, words, and letters. Frequently, by avoiding these words, sounds, and letters, you'll make statements you had not intended to make or reply to questions with totally irrelevant answers.

Another tactic you use to avoid saying these difficult words, sounds, or letters is to insert an introductory phrase that helps you delay saying the dreaded sound. This will often get you started talking without a block or a stutter. On other occasions, you hope that while expressing this introductory phrase, you'll think of a way to avoid the difficult word. At the very least, the introductory phrase will give you a chance to brace yourself for the coming struggle. At times, you won't be able to think of an introductory phrase so will insert a single word — e.g., "actually," "um," etc. — or you may cough as though clearing your throat.

**Get me out of here**

Many people who stutter — including you, perhaps — not

only avoid words, sounds, and letters, but also avoid participating in many life-enhancing opportunities. Many times you'll have something to say but won't say it — in the classroom, at a public meeting, or at social gatherings.

Most people, including people who do not stutter, have social anxiety from time to time and avoid speaking up in social situations. But this tendency seems to be exaggerated in people who stutter. Even when the stakes are high, such as when you have the opportunity to apply for a better job or to make the acquaintance of an attractive member of the opposite sex, you simply avoid the situation, keep your mouth shut, and miss out on a great opportunity.

Very often you will avoid taking a leadership role even if you have the necessary skills. You'll avoid jobs that involve a lot of public speaking or speaking on the phone. In short, you'll avoid anything that puts you in the limelight where there is a possibility that people will become aware of your stuttering and judge you negatively, or as an inferior human being. Because, in your own mind, you feel ashamed of your stuttering and judge yourself harshly, you assume that others are making the same judgment. And to you, that seems like a fate worse than death.

On the social scene, you'll turn down invitations to parties and resist joining organizations such as political parties or becoming active in your church.

The more important the situation and the greater your desire is to speak to someone, the more likely you are to feel anxious when talking to that person. This, in turn, causes you to stutter more in these situations. To avoid the embarrassment, you choose to avoid these anxiety-creating situations. In other words, the more you want to speak to someone, or the more important the situation, the more likely you are to remain silent or to avoid the situation entirely. Consequently, you miss out on countless life-enriching opportunities.

Avoiding these life-enhancing situations and not participating in life to its full extent is perhaps the highest price you pay for stuttering. Being fully alive and fully human means pursuing a life that is rewarding and joyful. When you avoid important situations and influential or attractive people, you lose the opportunity to gain what you want from life, you settle for second best, or even end up with the opposite of what you actually want.

## Feelings

People who stutter — as well as people who don't stutter — experience a wide range of emotions. These emotions were helpful and necessary in the early evolution of the human species. Some of our emotions are positive and joyful; they give meaning to the human experience. Other emotions are negative and very unpleasant; they rob us of a productive and gratifying experience.

As well as being pleasant or unpleasant, emotions can also be healthy or unhealthy. For the person who stutters, unhealthy negative emotions are an almost constant companion.

You might ask, "What's the difference between a healthy and an unhealthy negative emotion?" Healthy negative emotions (1) are non-extreme, (2) they help us to adjust to an undesirable situation or to change it, and (3) they recede once they are no longer needed. On the other hand, unhealthy negative emotions (1) tend to be extreme, (2) interfere with our adjustment to an unpleasant situation or any attempt to change it, and (3) they hang around long after their "use-by date" has expired. Simply put, unhealthy negative emotions prevent us from living life to the fullest in the most satisfying manner.

What are some of these unhealthy negative emotions?

As we've already seen, anxiety — especially social anxiety — plays a major part in the life of the person who stutters. Any time you come into contact with other human beings and are expected to speak with them, your anxiety level goes up.

Another common emotion is shame. You may feel ashamed if you stutter while speaking, or you may feel ashamed if you avoid talking to someone so as to hide the fact that you stutter. You may also feel guilty about your stuttering or about avoiding people.

Because you avoid many opportunities that are open to you, your life is not as fulfilling as it would otherwise be. When you compare your life to how it could be, you may feel depressed. Dwelling on the fact that life seems unfair or that you are ill-equipped to participate in much of life leads to deep despondency.

At other times, you may feel angry — angry at those who are unwilling or unable to accept you and your stuttering, and angry at the world because you stutter. You may even feel angry at yourself, and frequently turn that anger into a deep sense of guilt.

These unhealthy negative emotions add to the frustration of not speaking as fluently as you would like. In fact, these emotions frequently exacerbate your stuttering.

If, like many people who stutter, you've been trying for years to speak fluently but have been unable to do so consistently, especially if you've had speech therapy and temporarily improved your fluency, you would not be alone in feeling a deep sense of helplessness and hopelessness.

## The full picture

To accurately define and describe stuttering requires much more than a focus on its obvious visible and audible aspects. It is not enough to merely describe those characteristics of stuttering that an outside observer can see and hear. As well as the blocks and repetitions and noticeable body movements, there are many facets of stuttering that remain hidden. And in many cases, people who stutter, do all that they can to hide the fact that they stutter by avoiding people and situations. Any definition of stuttering that does not include thoughts, feelings, and actions — including hidden actions as well as actions that are designed to cover up the fact that you stutter — is incomplete.

Having a complete definition of stuttering has definite advantages if you are looking for a way to overcome stuttering and its lifestyle-inhibiting effects.

By being fully aware of the multi-dimensional nature of stuttering, you can start working on overcoming it from a variety of directions. You are not limited to improving your control over the biomechanics of speech. By attacking some of the emotional and behavioral aspects of stuttering directly, you can begin to live life more fully whether or not you increase your fluency.

Even if you continue to stutter as much as you currently do, if you can overcome your anxiety and shame, you can throw yourself into life and all it has to offer. Never again will you have to avoid situations that involve speaking. You'll be able to participate in public meetings, apply for the job you want, ask questions in class, and approach members of the opposite sex to ask them out on a date.

As a byproduct of living without shame and anxiety, and especially avoidances, you may find — although there are no guarantees — that you become more fluent. This is especially so if, like most people who began stuttering as a child, you're able to speak fluently — or at least more fluently — when no one else is around. If you don't stutter or are markedly more fluent when you're on your own, then the methods described in this book will probably help you to become more fluent in public. Even if there is no improvement in your fluency, the ideas and activities you'll learn in future chapters will definitely help you to have a more rewarding and joyful life.

**Remember this:**

- There are many aspects of lifelong stuttering that have absolutely nothing to do with speaking.

- By being fully aware of the multi-dimensional nature of stuttering, you can start working on overcoming it from a variety of directions.

# 5 WHY ME?

---

**In this chapter you will:**

- Learn about the different stages of developmental stuttering.

- Discover the important role of thinking habits.

---

## Understanding the causes of stuttering

Many of us who stutter want to know the cause of our stuttering. The question we ask is, "Why me?"

To understand the cause of stuttering, it's important to keep in mind that stuttering is more than just speech disfluency. As we saw in the previous chapter, stuttering often includes a wide range of feelings, thoughts, and actions: shame, depression, low self-esteem, blinking, twitching, avoiding words, and avoiding people, to name a few.

Here, for the first time, we outline a model that explains the cause of stuttering, including the feelings, attitudes, and actions that go along with speech disfluency. The model follows a timeline that begins before we are born and continues up to the present day. It shows that some of the causes of stuttering are beyond our control, and some are within our control.

## Stage one: In the beginning

Our very early ancestors lived in a physical and social environment that was significantly different from ours. As a result of their environment, people with a mindset that helped them to adapt to their conditions survived better than those who thought differently. Unfortunately for us, many of those previously helpful thinking habits are unhelpful in our environment. These thinking habits include a low tolerance for frustration and a tendency to demand changes in ourselves, others, and our environment. All humans, including those who stutter and those who do not, have inherited these thinking habits. However, people who stutter have probably inherited a stronger dose of these unhelpful thinking habits.

The crucial role that these thought patterns play in stuttering will become apparent in later stages of the model.

While all of us have inherited the genes that give rise to unhelpful attitudes and beliefs, many people who stutter may have inherited another gene — one that delays the acquisition of speech. Research shows that the delayed onset of speech stuttering is more common in people who stutter. For example, generally speaking, girls learn to speak earlier than boys. Learning to speak earlier may explain why fewer girls than boys stutter.

While we are developing in the womb, some of our genes are growing weaker, some stronger, some are forming clusters, and some stop working altogether. Which genes thrive and which do not is partly determined by the lifestyle of our mother. For example, poor nutrition, alcohol and drug abuse, as well as knocks to the body of our mother can all play a part in the prenatal development of our brain. Your mother's lifestyle is far from the sole determinant as to whether or not you'll stutter, but it does play a part in some cases.

As well as our genetic makeup, the inherent dangers of the birthing process can contribute to brain damage which leads to stuttering. These dangers include premature birth and oxygen deprivation as a result of becoming entangled in the umbilical cord.

So before we are 24 hours old, we may already be vulnerable to stuttering.

## Stage two: The early years

Although learning to speak comes naturally to us, like any skill, it takes time to master. Along the way, we will make many mistakes and stumble over our words. If our parents display some anxiety over our speaking errors, we may quickly learn that talking is dangerous and we must be vigilant to ensure we speak proficiently. Suddenly, talking becomes serious — deadly serious. The most important thing in the world becomes whether we succeed or fail at speaking fluently.

Our parents, who like everybody else on the planet are influenced by their ancestors' thinking genes, demand that their child must speak fluently. Unfortunately, many parents blame themselves for their child's stuttering. Or worse, they blame the child. Their ancient thinking habits lead them to conclude, "My child should be able to speak fluently."

Some parents become hypersensitive to all their child's

speaking errors and become more aware of them than other adults. They notice disfluencies in their child that other parents would overlook in their children.

Again, this does not mean that your parents cause you to stutter, but they can — and often do — influence the way you think and feel about stuttering, and about yourself. And as we've noted several times, thoughts and feelings are an integral part of the entire stuttering experience.

Picking up on the cues from our parents, plus a developing awareness of our own speaking difficulties, leads us to slap a label on ourselves: "I'm a stutterer." Our speech, instead of being a part of us, becomes who we are.

At about this point, our own genetic inheritance kicks in. We make demands on ourselves, "I must not stutter; I must have total control over my speech!" and our low tolerance for frustration has us concluding that "I can't stand this." These thoughts heighten our anxiety, which in turn increases our disfluency.

When we look around us, we notice that our peers don't share our difficulty talking. We grow increasingly aware of our parents' concerns about our speech and repeat our demand for change: "I should be able to speak normally like my friends."

Because we don't "speak normally like our friends" as we "should," we begin to see ourselves as deficient, a disappointment to our parents. Our self-esteem plummets and we erroneously conclude that we're inferior, worthless human beings. We learn to avoid other people so as to hide our shame. If we can't avoid people, then we try to avoid the words that most clearly reveal our deficiency and our "inferiority."

In a world where everyone is apparently "better than" us, we naturally feel afraid talking to our "superiors." Our fear prompts us to be more vigilant, to focus more intently on our speech and, paradoxically, to stutter more.

## Stage three: Habit

In our mind, we form an association between speech, danger, and anxiety. We can't think of talking without also thinking about danger. Because talking and danger "naturally" go together, we can't speak without fear. And for us, fear plus talking leads to stuttering.

In time, we discover that we can sometimes speak more fluently if we put in some effort and really struggle to get our words out. To the outside observer, it appears that we are fighting with our bodies to get the words out. Because our effort and struggle are sometimes rewarded with more fluent speech, struggling becomes a habit. Eventually, we can no longer speak without struggle and effort. Our struggling speech is further reinforced by our ancient thinking habit: "I can't stand being stuck; therefore I must struggle until I can force the word out."

On occasions, we notice that when we're stuck, we're sometimes able to become unstuck by blinking, jerking our head, or snapping our fingers, etc. We then superstitiously connect blinking and jerking with fluent speech and develop another habit: blinking, jerking, or finger-snapping until we can no longer speak without these bodily movements.

The fear and shame we feel when talking to others grows stronger, especially if we assume that they're looking down on us because of the "weird" things we do when we talk. We feel uncomfortable around others and our ancient genes tell us, "I can't stand this discomfort; I must avoid talking to people." So we avoid others as much as possible and feel a deep sense of relief. Unfortunately, we see the relief as a reward for avoiding others and, because we like rewards, our self-imposed social isolation becomes yet another habit.

Many people who stutter try therapy to overcome their stuttering. But therapy often fails — mainly because the therapy doesn't take into account the role of our inherited, ancient beliefs. But we see therapy's failure as our failure, "It's all my fault. I should be able to overcome this. I'm such a failure." This thinking adds to our sense of hopelessness and helplessness, and our stuttering becomes more entrenched.

For many people who stutter, despair turns to depression and outrage. The thinking habits we inherited from our early ancestors have us believing, "Life's not fair. This shouldn't happen to me. I deserve better than this. Other people should show more compassion towards me."

## Stage four: Beyond destiny

This model shows that stuttering and its causes are multi-faceted. It shows how various forces interact with one another to make stuttering deeply entrenched and to affect our lives in more ways than non-stutterers might imagine.

But the model also provides hope and a hint at what effective therapy might entail.

We can't undo the past and relive our time in the womb or our early childhood. But we can learn to be on the lookout for outdated thinking patterns and to replace them with a rigorous, modern scientific outlook that does away with ancient demands and the fear of frustration and discomfort. We can learn to accept ourselves as we are, and become more relaxed in our own skin.

In addition to fluency shaping, stuttering modification, and other evidence-based therapies, it's vital that we develop a more modern attitude towards ourselves and stuttering. This new attitude, without demands and low tolerance for frustration, allows us to become more accepting of ourselves, others, and life in general, including stuttering.

## Stuttering and self-acceptance

Here's the reality: you stutter now and you probably always will stutter, at least to some degree. But the news isn't all bad. Even though your stuttering will never go away completely, it's possible to reduce the frequency and — more importantly — the severity of your speech disfluency so no one notices that you stutter. The technical term for this level of fluency — where no one notices that you stutter — is *operational fluency*.

Because your stuttering will never go away completely, it's important to accept your stuttering, and accept yourself despite your stuttering, no matter how severe it is. Putting yourself down is a pointless waste of your time and energy. It not only causes you pain; it increases the severity and frequency of your stuttering, making it harder to develop operational fluency. When you accept yourself, you not only feel better, but your self-acceptance will help you to speak more fluently.

## Looking ahead

In the following chapters you'll learn the tools and develop the skills to gain operational fluency. You'll learn how to look at stuttering and yourself in a new light so you feel better about yourself. The primary tool in this new, modern approach to stuttering recovery is called Rational Emotive Behavior Therapy (REBT). We'll show you what REBT is and how it works. Additionally, we'll show you ways to directly manipulate your speech. Throughout the remaining chapters, you'll have an opportunity to start practicing REBT and speech manipulation. REBT combined with direct speech manipulation will set you on the path to operational fluency.

> **Remember this:**
>
> - Stuttering has more than one cause.
>
> - Thinking habits play a vital role in the cause and prevention of stuttering.
>
> - Most stuttering therapies fail.
>
> - You'll probably never be a perfect speaker, but you can learn to decrease the frequency and severity of your stuttering and develop operational fluency.
>
> - Operational fluency comes from combining acceptance of stuttering, self-acceptance, and direct speech manipulation.

# 6 HOW TO CONQUER SHAME AND FEAR

---

**In this chapter you will:**

- Discover the real cause of emotions.

- Learn how to change your feelings.

---

## Shame and fear

In previous chapters, we saw that there is more to stuttering than speech disfluency. People who stutter also deal with strong, unpleasant, unhealthy emotions, particularly anxiety and shame. In this chapter, you'll discover the real cause of anxiety, shame, and other emotions. Hint: it's not stuttering.

When I (G.N.) was a young man in college, I felt deeply ashamed of my stutter. Because I was ashamed, I avoided parties and other social occasions. Whenever I spoke to someone, I refused to make eye contact with them. One of my goals in life was to teach in college, but I forfeited that goal because I felt so ashamed and inadequate. When I left college, I passed up opportunities to pursue management positions for which I was well-qualified.

Along with shame, I felt incredibly anxious. I was afraid that every time I opened my mouth, no sound would come out. Paradoxically, the harder I tried to speak without stuttering, the more I stuttered and the more anxious I felt. I would tense my lips, blink my eyes, and jerk my head. But my stuttering just got worse and my anxiety intensified.

As if stuttering were not bad enough, shame and anxiety add to our suffering. Not only do shame and anxiety feel bad, but almost always, these emotions make us even less fluent. Worse yet, they lead us to make life choices that limit our experiences and hold us back from reaching our full potential.

## Where do feelings come from?

What causes all this suffering? Does our stuttering make us feel anxious and ashamed or is it something else? Could it be our childhood or other experiences we've had in life that create our emotions? Perhaps we're born that way? All of these things contribute, in some way, to our feelings. But they are not the main cause. So what is the main cause of shame and anxiety?

Quite simply, it's the way we think. Some thoughts will make you anxious, some will make you ashamed, and some will make you angry. Speaking at a public meeting will not make you anxious; and stuttering does not make you feel ashamed. Your thoughts about speaking at a public meeting make you anxious; and your thoughts about stuttering make you feel ashamed.

If it were true that speaking at a public meeting caused you to feel anxious, then everyone who spoke at public meetings would experience anxiety. Yet we know that everyone does not feel anxious when they speak up in public. Some people enjoy the experience. Even people who stutter do not all feel anxious when they speak up at a public meeting. And among those who do feel anxious, some experience high levels of anxiety, some have moderate levels of anxiety, and others have only mild anxiety. Similarly, not everyone who stutters feels ashamed of their stuttering. And those people who do feel ashamed of their stuttering experience different levels of shame.

The reason for these differences is that people hold different points of view about speaking in public and about stuttering in general. It's these differences of opinion that lead to differences in feelings.

You may notice that your anxiety is sometimes much stronger than at other times, or that the depth of your shame varies from time to time. What causes this variation? Your feelings change when you change what you tell yourself about speaking in public and what you tell yourself about stuttering. Any time you have an emotional change it is because you have changed the way you talk to yourself.

Our emotions are an integral part of the holistic view of stuttering that we have presented in previous chapters. Any full definition of stuttering includes emotions such as shame and anxiety. And now we find that we create our emotions. Shame and anxiety are not products of stuttering, they are products of our thinking. So let's take a closer look at these two troubling emotions and see what, if anything, we can do with them. We'll begin with shame.

## Understanding shame

Shame is an emotion you experience when you don't feel good about yourself. It begins when you do something that you believe publicly reveals one of your weaknesses or defects. Perhaps you regard your stuttering as a weakness or defect and you feel ashamed whenever you stutter in public. Shame — often accompanied by guilt — can also occur when you think you have let down people who are important to you. Some people who stutter think that they are letting down family members or work colleagues whenever they stutter. Shame can also occur when you think people are — in your opinion, rightly — looking down on you and judging you negatively. You may feel ashamed after you stutter in public and assume that others think less of you for being unable to speak fluently.

It's important to remember that your shame does not come from having your weaknesses revealed, or having let down important people, or having others look down on you. Your shame comes from the things you tell yourself about these circumstances.

What type of thoughts lead to shame? The two key thinking styles that lead to shame are (1) having rigid views of what you should and shouldn't do, and (2) thinking less of yourself for not living up to your rigid ideals.

It is the combination of inflexible, rigid rules and judging yourself negatively that leads to shame. Therefore, we can say that shame comes from believing that you must not have a weakness or defect or else you're inferior; it comes from believing that you must not let down important people or else you're no good; and it comes from believing that you must not give people a reason to look down on you or else you're inadequate.

These rigid beliefs tend to cloud your judgment about yourself, other people, and shame in general. When you find yourself in a situation where you could do or have done something which you regard as shameful, you tend to overestimate (1) the shamefulness of your shortcomings, (2) the extent to which others will notice your shortcomings, (3) the likelihood that others will regard your shortcomings as shameful, (4) the length of time that others will think about and remember your shortcomings, and (5) the extent to which news of your shortcomings will travel. When you make yourself vulnerable to shame, you tend to regard the world as a dangerous place where — at any moment — you could fail to live up to your rigid ideals and have your defects exposed.

Because shame is such an unpleasant emotion to experience, you do all that you can to avoid it. But in your effort to avoid shame, it can take over your life and rule the way you live. When you allow shame to rule your life, you move away and withdraw from others, you fail to make eye contact with the people you meet, you stick to yourself and avoid socializing or advancing your career, and you try to overcompensate for your shortcomings by pushing yourself mercilessly to be exceptional in other areas of your life.

## Say goodbye to shame

The good news is that it doesn't have to be this way. Because you create shame with the way you talk to yourself, you can eliminate it by changing the way you talk yourself. You wrote the script that makes you feel ashamed; therefore you have the power to change the script.

What changes will get rid of shame? You'll recall that shame comes from having rigid views on what you must and must not do, and thinking less of yourself for not living up to your rigid ideals. Therefore, you can eliminate your shame by developing more flexible views and by refraining from judging yourself negatively.

Here is a question for you: do you have to speak fluently? Think about it. Is there a law of the universe that says you must speak fluently and must not stutter? If you think about it carefully, you can't fail to arrive at the conclusion that there is no law that says you must speak fluently or that you must not stutter. Yet you've been telling yourself the exact opposite for years. You have convinced yourself that you have to speak fluently. Each time you open your mouth to speak, in the back of your mind is a voice that says "I must not have a repetition or block, I need to speak fluently." Of course, when you speak, you break your own rule and stutter. And then the self-downing begins, "I should have spoken fluently; I'm such a loser." No wonder you feel ashamed.

Now imagine if you changed the script. Instead of insisting on fluency, try giving yourself permission to stutter. Instead of saying, "I must not stutter," tell yourself, "it's okay to stutter; there is no law of the universe that says I must be perfectly fluent." Assuming you genuinely believe this new script, do you really think you would feel ashamed of your speech? What is there to be ashamed of? By giving yourself permission to stutter, you absolve yourself from any wrongdoing, and you have no reason to put yourself down. Which brings us to the second key component of shame: self downing.

When you put yourself down, you don't merely disapprove of your actions or your speech, you disapprove of your entire self. You believe you are a weak, defective person. You see yourself as an inadequate person, someone who is not good enough, or someone who is disgusting. It isn't merely your behavior or your speech which is a problem, you are a problem.

This type of thinking overlooks what it means to be human. As a human being, you are a complex organism with a variety of different behaviors, feelings, thoughts, accomplishments, personality traits, hopes and dreams, as well as many body parts. When you rate your entire self as defective because your speech is disfluent, you lump all of these components together and declare that none of them has any value. It's as though one part of you equals all of you. Rejecting your entire self because you dislike one or two characteristics is like throwing out an entire bowl of fruit merely because one or two grapes have gone rotten. It makes no sense.

The remedy for self-downing is to separate the part from the whole. By all means you can rate your stuttering as an inconvenience; you can even hate your stuttering. But by separating your stuttering from the whole of you, you can accept and approve of yourself while disliking or disapproving of your stuttering.

When you acknowledge that you don't have to speak fluently and accept yourself when you stutter, your shame will disappear. Instead of putting yourself down and feeling ashamed, you can show yourself the same compassion you would demonstrate towards any other human being you see struggling with a part of life they find difficult. The concept of self-acceptance is such an important one that we have devoted an entire chapter to it (see chapter 8).

Let's now turn our attention from shame to anxiety.

## Understanding anxiety

Anxiety is an unpleasant emotion you experience when you face a situation that you regard as dangerous or threatening. Broadly speaking, there are two types of threatening situations where you could experience anxiety: (1) situations where you might be inconvenienced or uncomfortable; and (2) situations where your self-image or sense of self-worth might be threatened.

People who stutter often perceive speaking as a dangerous or threatening situation. It presents two threats. Firstly, there is the threat that you'll feel uncomfortable. This is especially so if you experience shame about your speech. You can also feel threatened by the discomfort of anxiety itself. Secondly, there is a threat to your self-image or sense of self-worth if you perceive that people around you are looking down on you because of your speech.

Your anxiety does not come from the threats you face, whether they be threats to your comfort or your self-image. You make yourself feel anxious by the things you tell yourself about those threats.

What type of thoughts lead to anxiety? The three key thinking styles that lead to anxiety are (1) overestimating the harm the threat will inflict upon you, (2) underestimating your ability to cope with the threat, and (3) demanding that you avoid or avert the threat.

Once again, we see that inflexible demands (in this case, the demand that you avoid or avert the threat) combine with faulty evaluations to create your anxiety. Therefore, your anxiety comes from believing that whatever you are threatened with is unbearable and must be avoided or averted; if it were to happen, it would be the end of the world, a fate worse than death.

These demands and evaluations distort your views of the world. You obsess or constantly think about the threat you could be facing; you see threats where they don't exist and feel certain that they will trip you up; and you regard slightly threatening situations as extremely dangerous.

Because anxiety feels so uncomfortable, you do all that you can to avoid it. But the steps you take to avoid anxiety reduce your quality of life. For example, you avoid situations where you might need to speak to strangers. If you can't avoid the situation, then you try to remain silent once you get there. As with shame, this leads to self-limiting life choices such as not applying for a promotion or avoiding conversations with attractive members of the opposite sex.

## Kiss your fears goodbye

Again, we have good news. Because you create your own anxiety with your demands and faulty evaluations, you can eradicate your anxiety by developing more flexible views and more accurate evaluations of the threat and your ability to cope with it.

Unquestionably, stuttering is an inconvenience; it gets in the way of clear, concise communication. But is it fatal? Will you die merely because your speech does not flow as fluently and as smoothly as you would like? Hardly! It might take you longer to get the words out, but no one is going to die of malnutrition waiting for them — least of all you. Certainly, no one would choose to be a person who stutters. But is it the worst thing that could possibly happen to you? There are far greater calamities in life than repetitions and blocks. Similarly, having others reject you or look down on you is unpleasant but it's not the end of the world.

You may need to accept discomfort and rejection as a natural part of life — there is no reason why you must be exempt from these misfortunes. Unfortunately, the world does not operate according to our dictates. You can't just demand that discomfort and rejection not exist and have them magically disappear.

Additionally, you don't have to feel good — free of shame and anxiety — all the time. In fact, striving to constantly feel good is an exercise in futility and ignores the reality that life is often difficult. The harder you try to avoid discomfort and rejection, the more anxious you'll make yourself and less challenges you'll confront.

## Do you stutter more severely because of this mistake?

Many people make the mistake of trying to hide the fact that they stutter. The avoidance strategies employed include: struggling and trying to force themselves to speak fluently; using starter words; avoiding certain sounds; substitution; circumlocution; inserting pauses; and remaining silent as much as possible. This strategy of avoidance often backfires because it makes you more anxious about stuttering, which increases your disfluency. Additionally, your sense of shame increases when you are in a situation where you can't remain silent and are forced to reveal your stutter. Put simply, attempting to hide your stutter is counterproductive — it only makes things worse for you.

A far better strategy is to stutter openly, making no attempt to hide your disfluency. If you feel overwhelmed by this idea, you can treat it as an experiment. Try it for a while and see what happens.

You can prove to yourself that stuttering and rejection are not fatal by deliberately stuttering and observing the results. When you stutter voluntarily without making any attempt to speak fluently, you'll see that nothing catastrophic happens. Some people may react discourteously toward you, but their actions will almost certainly cause you no physical harm.

Another experiment you can try is to advertise the fact that you stutter. Instead of trying to hide it, tell people you meet, right away, that you stutter. When you advertise your speech disfluency in this way, very often you'll find that people treat you kindly rather than reject you. Even if they do reject you, you can stand it — you won't die from their rejection.

By confronting your fears and facing up to them squarely, you can knock them down to size so that they no longer bother you. The more exposure you have to the things you fear, the less reason you'll have to fear them. As you confront your fears, remind yourself that they are not fatal and that you will survive. Don't forget to remind yourself that you can cope with your feelings — especially shame and anxiety — they won't kill you.

Fear and shame can be debilitating emotions. But you don't have to live with them. You can conquer them by adopting flexible, non-demanding attitudes and non-exaggerated views. You can cement these new attitudes by confronting your fears and stuttering openly.

In this chapter, we've seen how certain ideas lead to shame and anxiety. You have discovered that, by modifying those ideas, you can overcome crippling emotions that increase the severity of your stuttering and hold you back from leading a rich and fulfilling your life. In the next chapter, will look at more disabling ideas that interfere with your speech and prevent you from reaching you're full potential. You'll also learn some strategies to override these ideas and break free from the restraints holding you back.

---

**Remember this:**

- Shame and anxiety contribute to stuttering.

- You feel the way you think.

- You can change your feelings by changing your thinking.

---

## 7 THE FREEDOM TO BE YOU

In this chapter you will:

- See how your beliefs contribute to your stuttering.
- Learn to recognize some of the most common irrational beliefs that lead to stuttering.

## Are you making the most of your life?

Take a look around you. Everyone you see — whether or not they stutter — was born and raised with a tendency to think irrationally, to believe ideas that simply are not true. You are no exception.

As you learned in the previous chapter, this tendency to think irrationally, which we all seem to have inherited from our ancient ancestors, leads you to experience unhealthy negative emotions and to act in ways that are not in your best interests. As a result, you frequently don't make the most of your opportunities and so live a life that is less than optimal.

Because you are human, you are motivated by short-range goals (enjoying yourself while avoiding pain and discomfort) as well as long-range goals (making the most of your life and reaching your full potential). Long-range and short-range goals often conflict with one another forcing you to choose between them. For example, your short-range goal of avoiding talking to strangers may conflict with your long-range goal of applying for a better job. Optimal living requires that you balance these competing goals to lead a long, healthy, and happy life in peaceful and cooperative harmony with others, surrounded by friends and loved ones.

Human nature ensures that you will often think and act in ways that significantly interfere with your goals and prevent you from feeling happy or fulfilled. In the above example, you may choose not to apply for a more satisfying job, thereby ensuring that you remain in your current job which you thoroughly dislike. To some extent, your life is a battleground where rational and irrational ideas compete for supremacy. Because rational and irrational ideas have equal strength, the battle will never end and will persist throughout your life.

Let's now look at some common irrational beliefs and see how they not only interfere with your quality of life, but also contribute to your disfluency.

## Idea number 1

*I need to be liked and loved: Everyone must like me and approve of me. I must not be rejected or looked down upon.*

There is nothing wrong with wanting people to like you and approve of you. But wanting approval becomes a problem when you insist on it and consider it a necessity. The need for approval makes you anxious and restricts your life because you're overly concerned with what other people think of you. If you're afraid that others will look down on you and reject you because of the way you talk, you avoid taking risks, and even avoid talking to people altogether. The irony is, the more you isolate yourself from others, the fewer friends you'll have and the less reason people will have to like and admire you.

The key to getting over your approval addiction is to recognize that approval, while highly desirable, is not a need. The idea that we don't need approval seems to fly in the face of everything we've been told, doesn't it? But here's another way of looking at it.

What would happen to you if you were locked in a room without oxygen or water? You would die, right? The fact is, you need oxygen and water. But what would happen to you if you were locked in a room without approval? Would you die? Hardly! The fact is, you don't need approval. You can survive without it.

But would you be happy? Probably, you would not be as happy as you would be if people liked and admired you. But you could be happy nevertheless. There are hundreds of things you can do and enjoy without needing anyone to tell you what a wonderful person you are. You don't need anyone's approval to enjoy a movie; to enjoy learning to play a musical instrument; to enjoy playing or watching a sport; to create or appreciate art; to enjoy a good meal; to immerse yourself in a humanitarian project; or to enjoy the wonders of nature and the cosmos, etc.

Having someone criticize you or look down on you because of your stutter is unpleasant but it's not fatal. You can stand their disapproval. People have looked down on you in the past, and you're still alive. Get into the habit of reminding yourself that you don't need approval and start living the life you want to lead, regardless of what others think of you.

The reality is you don't need to be liked or loved: Significant people in your life don't have to like you and approve of you; they can — and, from time to time, probably will — reject you or look down on you.

## Idea number 2

*I must be competent: I must be able to do anything that any other human being can do. I mustn't make mistakes or look foolish and I must hide my inadequacies.*

No one is perfect; all of us are imperfect and fallible. Along with our strengths, we all have many weaknesses. When you deny yourself the right to have blocks and repetitions, or to make mistakes or be flawed in any way, you deny yourself the right to be human. The more you insist on perfect fluency, and the more you try to cover up the fact that you stutter, the more anxious you'll become, which will only make it harder for you to speak fluently. Your insistence on perfect fluency will discourage you from taking on challenges and experiencing all that life has to offer. By demanding complete fluency or hiding the fact that you stutter, you make yourself anxious, and this tension can harm not only your relationships and limit your opportunities, but it can also harm your health.

Fluency is worth striving for, but turning it into a necessity merely adds to your anxiety and makes you less fluent. Despite your best efforts, whenever you strive for perfect fluency, the parts of your body that control your speech will frequently let you down and you will stutter. Making yourself upset won't improve your speech. Instead of demanding fluency, give yourself permission to stutter. Ironically, you may find that when you allow yourself the freedom to stutter, you become more fluent.

As with approval, you don't need to be perfectly fluent. Total fluency is desirable but it is not a necessity. You can survive, and lead a long and healthy, happy life no matter how much you stutter. Your speech difficulties are no reason to give up on yourself or to give up on making the most of your life.

You don't have to be competent: you don't have to be able to do things just because everyone else can. You are allowed to make mistakes or look foolish and there's no need to hide your inadequacies.

## Idea number 3

*I must have my own way: I must get what I want when I want it. There are some things in life I shouldn't have to put up with.*

It makes sense to want things to turn out the way you would like them to be, so naturally it makes sense to want to speak fluently. Unfortunately, you often go beyond merely wanting fluency and believe you *must* speak fluently. As a result, you have a very low tolerance for your speech difficulties and find yourself getting angry at yourself — or the world — whenever you stutter.

By insisting that you not be frustrated by disfluent speech, you only add to your frustration each time you stutter. If, instead, you learn to accept the frustration of repetitions and blocks you will probably continue to feel some disappointment about your speech, but you'll no longer feel angry or self-pitying.

You can learn to accept the frustration of stuttering by recognizing that there is no law of the universe that says you must be exempt from frustration or that you must speak fluently. None of us is immune from frustration, and your speech difficulties are just one of the frustrations that appear on this planet. Such is life. Jumping up and down, screaming blue bloody murder or complaining about the unfairness of it all, won't change a thing.

You don't have to get your own way: you can get by without having what you want when you want it. There are some unpleasant things in life you will just have to put up with.

## Idea number 4

*People must do what's right: People who do anything wrong, especially if they harm me, are evil and they deserve to be punished.*

It's an unfortunate fact of life that some people will be prejudiced against you because of your speech. They may refuse to date you, or turn you down for a job or a promotion which you could easily handle. Others may ridicule you or gossip about your speech behind your back. No one can be certain what causes them to act this way. Perhaps they don't know any better and don't know how to react politely and compassionately toward you. Or maybe they are emotionally or psychologically disturbed and have a nasty, cruel streak.

Expecting and demanding respect is a recipe for misery because it leads to anger and anxiety. Sadly, few people will change their behavior merely because you demand it. Much as we would like it, people do not have to treat us kindly and fairly. Although common decency suggests they will treat you with courtesy and respect, courtesy and respect are not compulsory — there is no universal law compelling people to act decently. People have a right to choose — for whatever reason, no matter how unjustified — to treat you with disrespect. The universe, and the people in it, are not required to act according to your expectations and demands — regardless of how justified you are.

People don't have to do what's right: People who misbehave, even if they harm you, are not evil. Unless punishment teaches them to act differently (which it seldom does), it serves little purpose.

## Idea number 5

*I must be safe: I must avoid threatening situations especially if they make me feel uncomfortable or make me look inadequate or inferior.*

The world is a dangerous place so it pays to be on the alert for dangers — speeding cars, falling objects, violent people, etc — and to avoid them as best you can. But some "dangers" are not dangerous at all — the inconvenience of being passed over for a job or promotion, or having people think less of you because of the way you speak, for example.

Very often the thing you fear is not stuttering or the rejection and contempt of others. What you really fear is how you will feel when you stutter or when you are rejected.

When you regard non-life-threatening situations as dangerous, you tend to worry about them instead of facing them, and feel nervous and tense even though there is no real physical danger. This anxiety discourages you from doing the things you want to do, so you decline party invitations, and avoid applying for promotions at work.

To overcome your disabling fears, it's vital that you recognize that the things you are afraid of are not fatal — they won't kill you. Worrying about the things you fear won't make them magically disappear.

You don't have to be safe: you can face difficult situations, and almost certainly survive, even if you feel uncomfortable or look inadequate or inferior.

## Idea number 6

*Life should be easy: Nothing should go wrong in life. If there is a problem, there must be a quick and easy solution.*

Naturally, you'd like to find an effective and efficient way to stop stuttering. It's quite rational to have such a desire. However, you could very easily create a problem for yourself by changing your desire for a cure into a demand. It's quite possible that there will never be a cure for stuttering that comes with a 100% guarantee, although there may be numerous ways to make your stuttering less severe. If you insist on a perfect cure, then you may miss out on many of the methods that will improve your fluency.

By demanding a perfect cure, with a 100% guarantee of effectiveness, you'll be constantly dissatisfied with the methods that are available to improve your fluency, possibly without even trying them, resulting in no improvement in your fluency and a dissatisfaction with life in general.

Life doesn't have to be easy: Things can and will go wrong in life. If there is a problem, there is rarely a quick and easy solution, nor does there have to be.

## Idea number 7

*I am a victim: I can't help the way I feel. It's my problems, especially my stuttering, and other people that make me feel bad.*

Most of us feel happy when good things happen to us and unhappy when bad things happen. Reactions like these seem natural and normal; they are so common that many people assume that the events cause the emotional reactions. But do they?

People don't all react the same way to the same event. For example, you might be happy after a certain politician is elected, but other people feel unhappy over the same result. What causes this emotional variation? Quite simply, it's not the election result that makes you happy — it's your view or opinion of the result that makes you happy.

All of your reactions to life's events — unless you are under the influence of mind-altering drugs or have a brain injury or disorder — are the result of your view of those events. First, something happens (or you think it might happen). Second, you form an opinion of the situation. And third, you respond with feelings and actions that are determined by your opinion.

Rather than being at the mercy of what happens to you, you are at the mercy of your opinion of events. The significance of this fact cannot be overstated. By monitoring and adjusting your opinion of circumstances — including your opinion of stuttering — you can alter the way you feel and the way you act. For example, if you view stuttering as an unmitigated catastrophe and evidence of your unworthiness, you will probably feel depressed and avoid talking to people. But if you alter your view of stuttering and see it as a mere inconvenience that says nothing about your personal worth, you may feel sad and disappointed with your speech, but you won't be depressed and will freely interact with others.

You are not a victim: you can change the way you feel. It's not your problems and other people that make you feel bad; you make yourself feel bad by forming extreme opinions of events and circumstances.

## Idea number 8

*I must avoid problems: It's easier to ignore or run away from problems than it is to face them or try and solve them.*

Imagine you've been asked to give a speech to a local business group. You agree to give the talk even though you'd rather someone else gave it. As the day of the speech draws closer, you grow increasingly nervous. On the morning of the day you are due to give the speech, you feel so nervous that you phone the event organizer and falsely tell her you're sick and can't make it. She offers you her sympathies and wishes you a speedy recovery. When you hang up the phone, you feel an immediate sense of relief.

While the relief you feel at avoiding the speech feels good for a while, it doesn't help you to overcome your fear of talking to others. Additionally, you feel guilty for lying and letting down the event organizer, and you see yourself as inferior and inadequate for being unable to speak in front of the group. Eventually, you realize that the short-term benefits of avoiding the speech are outweighed by the long-term disadvantages. Had you given the speech, you may have felt uncomfortable, but you would not have had to lie and you would have proven to yourself that you are capable of giving a speech. Moreover, the relief and euphoria of having given the speech would have been far greater than the relief you felt at avoiding it.

Running away from for avoiding problems doesn't solve them. Often it makes them worse. If you allow your fear of speaking to control you so that you avoid talking to others, your fear will grow stronger. On the other hand, if you don't let the fear control you and speak up whenever you have the opportunity, you will eventually lose your fear. The more you speak to others, the easier it becomes.

You don't have to avoid problems: In the long run, it's easier to face them or try and solve problems than it is to ignore them or run away.

## Idea number 9

*I can't change: I am in the way I am today because of what has happened to me in the past; there's nothing I can do to change.*

Events in your past and in your childhood influence the way you feel and behave in the present. But not in the way you may think. Your personal history helped to shape your current belief system, the way you evaluate and view life's events. It is this current belief system, shaped in the past and subscribed to in the present, that causes you to feel and act the way you do today.

You can't change the past but you can change your beliefs. You can change your beliefs about the past, the present, and the future. Your past does not have to determine your present or your future. You can take charge of your life by re-evaluating the beliefs you formed in the past, keeping those beliefs which are true and helpful, and rejecting unhelpful, false beliefs. In particular, by rejecting beliefs that lead to extreme and rigid views of the present — including your view of your present speech — you can create a new life for yourself where you are no longer held back by fear and shame.

In the past, you may have formed the belief that you should be able to speak fluently, and that stuttering proves you are inferior. However, today you can reject that belief. You can easily justify the belief that there is no law of the universe requiring you to speak fluently and that your speech — whether fluent or disfluent — has no bearing on your personal worth.

You can change the way you respond to life: you are the way you are today, not so much because of what has happened to you in the past, but because of your current thoughts which you can always change.

## Take control of your life

Unfortunately, you can never rid yourself completely of the irrational ideas you inherited and had reinforced during your childhood. The greatest influence on your life is your genetic makeup. It is your genetic makeup that determines which beliefs will have the most influence over you, as well as ensuring that irrational beliefs will continue to influence you to some degree — despite your best efforts — for your entire life.

Because your biological makeup determines your beliefs, you don't have complete control over them. But you can control the degree — and to some extent, the frequency — of their influence over you. In fact, with hard work, persistence, and determination you can change your basic personality by (1) taking deliberate control of your conscious thoughts, (2) forcefully rejecting unhelpful, irrational ideas, and (3) resolutely affirming and nurturing mature, rational ideas.

Because of your biological, geographical, and social circumstances, there is a limit to what you can achieve in life. But within those limits, you have the freedom to choose how to think, feel, and act towards achieving fulfillment and happiness. You are not a puppet manipulated by outside circumstances. You choose your behavior, your thoughts, and — by extension — your feelings. Your thoughts, feelings, and actions are inseparable; they influence and interact with one another so that a change in one brings about a change in the other two. Because you can choose which thoughts to dwell on, and because those thoughts influence your feelings and actions, you can choose how you feel and how you act. Similarly, because you can control your actions, you can reinforce the way you think and the way you feel. In effect, you can construct — and reconstruct — the direction and the quality of your life.

Further, these internal factors — your thoughts, feelings, and actions — play a major role in determining external factors. Your world, and everything in it, is shaped by your opinions. Because of your highly personal, subjective point of view, you'll regard some situations as desirable and others as undesirable. Whether you move towards or shy away from situations depends on your view of those situations. The circumstances you find yourself in today are largely determined by your opinion-based reactions to the circumstances you found yourself in yesterday, which were, in turn, determined by your opinion of earlier events, and so on, ad infinitum. More importantly, you can shape tomorrow's circumstances by the view you take of today's circumstances.

The stronger your opinion of a situation, the stronger your reaction to it; extreme opinions lead to extreme — and often self-defeating — reactions. Therefore, if you are upset over an event, you'll get better results by changing your view of the event than from trying to change the event itself. This is especially true when the circumstances are unchangeable.

By training yourself to recognize common irrational beliefs and exchange them for more rational beliefs, you can be happier and live a more enriched life. The more effort you put into eliminating unhelpful thoughts from your consciousness (especially demands and exaggerated, overgeneralized complaints) and replacing them with helpful ideas, the greater freedom you have to reach your goals and your full potential. With determination and effort, you can override unhelpful ideas and act on helpful alternatives. When you act on mature ideas, you can choose values, goals, and ideals for yourself, as well as think and act in ways that best help you to achieve those goals.

## The benefits of thinking rationally

Learning to recognize unhelpful, untrue beliefs and replacing them with rational alternatives can dramatically improve your quality of life. Here just some of the ways that you can benefit from thinking rationally.

You will do more for yourself. Hopefully, you won't ignore the interests of others, but to a large extent you will put your own goals front and center. This is the only life you're likely to have, so it is important that you take care of yourself and make the most of life's opportunities. When you think rationally, you can decide what you want to do with your life and then do whatever it takes to reach your goals.

You will stop isolating yourself and join with others to get involved in community projects that help to make your community a better place in which to live, creating the kind of world in which you can thrive. One of life's great pleasures is surrounding yourself with a network of close friends. As you build your network of friends, you'll find that by working together synergistically, you can help build a better society — and have fun in the process. As people get to know you better, they will overlook the fact that you stutter and will concentrate on your other qualities.

With less concern for what others think of you, you'll be able to choose the direction of your own life and do the things you want to do. You can put yourself in the driver's seat and decide for yourself what you're going to do with your life. From time to time, you may make mistakes and regret some of your decisions. But rather than putting yourself down to your mistakes, you'll learn from them and become a stronger, more fulfilled human being.

You'll develop a greater tolerance for your flaws as well as for the flaws of others and won't make yourself miserable over things outside your control, including your predisposition to stuttering. You'll give yourself and others the right to be wrong, the right to be fallible, and the right to be human. You'll stop putting yourself down and condemning yourself.

You'll become more flexible and less demanding. You'll be able to bend with the wind instead of foolishly trying to stop it. You'll be open-minded and willing to change your beliefs and to take on challenges you never thought possible.

You'll be more accepting of uncertainty, fascinated by the exciting possibilities that life has to offer. Instead of insisting on a guarantee that you'll be able to speak fluently, you'll be willing to take a gamble and speak up on any occasion.

Instead of being self-absorbed, constantly fretting over your speech, you'll look beyond yourself and get more involved in life, committing yourself to creative pursuits that will benefit others as well as yourself. By throwing yourself into life, you'll look for ways to enhance your long-term health and happiness.

You'll develop an objective, realistic outlook that also considers the upside, and not just the downside, of communicating freely and openly with others. You'll be able to assess opportunities realistically and objectively and won't be deterred by irrational beliefs that have held you back in the past. Additionally, you will think more for yourself rather than relying on the opinions of others.

Instead of seeing life as a danger zone, you'll see it as an adventure. Without being foolhardy, you'll take risks and go after the things you want, even though you fully accept the possibility that you could fail. By taking chances and risking failure, you'll put yourself in a position to reach your goals at work and on the social scene.

You'll begin to focus on your long-term happiness. Instead of taking the quick, easy route that leads to long-term frustration and disappointment, you'll be willing to put up with some short-term discomfort and inconvenience in order to satisfy your long-term ambitions. For example, you'll put up with the short-term discomfort of talking to strangers in order to increase your social network and improve your career prospects.

You'll be more accepting of the fact that there is no heaven on earth and you're unlikely to get everything you want or avoid all discomfort and pain. You'll push yourself to pursue what's possible — a joyful, meaningful existence — without chasing a non-existent utopia, where everything is perfect.

You'll stop blaming life or other people for your woes, and take responsibility for the way you feel and the things you do. Instead of being a victim, you'll think for yourself while proactively and decisively choosing how to feel and what to do.

You'll accept yourself, warts and all. Instead of putting yourself down because of your speech difficulties, you'll focus on enjoying life rather than trying to prove yourself. You'll show yourself the same compassion you would to any other human being struggling with the hassles of day-to-day existence. You'll develop a growing confidence in the idea that although your speech may be disfluent, you are not a second rate human being.

Learning to accept yourself and giving yourself permission to be a fallible human being who stutters is such an important skill that we've devoted the next chapter entirely to showing you how to develop the habit of unconditional self-acceptance.

---

**Remember this:**

- Your beliefs contribute to your stuttering.

- Replacing irrational beliefs with their rational alternatives will dramatically increase your quality of life.

# 8 UNCONDITIONAL SELF-ACCEPTANCE

**In this chapter you will:**

- Learn about the harm you do to yourself by putting yourself down.

- See why self-esteem doesn't help — there is a better alternative.

## Self-Downing

Imagine that a new wonder drug has been developed. This new drug will make you happier, give you more self-confidence, allow you to be yourself, and prevent you from feeling inferior or afraid of rejection — no matter how much you stutter. This new drug begins working as soon as you take it and has no unpleasant side effects. Now imagine that this drug doesn't cost any money and you can take it as many times a day as you need. It sounds exciting, doesn't it? Would you take this drug?

The good news is, this miracle drug is available right

now — and you can start taking it today. It's called unconditional self-acceptance. The difference between unconditional self-acceptance (USA) and medication is that USA is not a drug — it's an attitude, a way of thinking about yourself. You can have unconditional self-acceptance today. All you have to do is to choose it, decide that that from now on you will accept yourself no matter what.

Unfortunately, most people who stutter do not accept themselves. Instead, they put themselves down and consider themselves inferior and inadequate human beings. Perhaps you have this tendency yourself. Here's how it works.

First, you hear yourself stutter and decide that you don't like stuttering. Next, you over generalize and decide that because you don't like stuttering, you don't like yourself. Because, as you see it, your stuttering is bad, therefore you are bad. Finally, because you regard yourself as inferior and inadequate, you assume that everyone else has the same negative opinion of you.

## How to recognize self-downing

When you put yourself down, you experience unhealthy, negative emotions such as anxiety and depression. Without giving it a second thought, you believe you are inadequate or inferior. Because of your self-downing, you isolate yourself from others and avoid opportunities to advance your career or to pursue loving relationships. Your self-downing leads you to think about yourself in prejudiced ways; you have a bias against yourself.

## The cost of self-downing

Self-downing leads to unhealthy negative emotions. The most common unhealthy, negative emotion you will experience is anxiety. Because you regard yourself as inadequate, you will be afraid of being rejected and criticized by others because of your stuttering. Your anxiety will prompt you to avoid speaking in public whenever possible. When you're unable to avoid speaking, you will be self-conscious and fearful of looking foolish.

Your self-downing can make you feel depressed. As you frequently reprimand yourself with statements such as, "I am worthless," or "I'm useless," you'll reinforce your negative opinion of yourself and begin to see yourself as undeserving and unlikable.

Your sense of inadequacy and inferiority will tend to make you feel ashamed. Whenever you stutter, you put yourself down, assume that your listeners also regard you negatively, and feel ashamed of your disfluent speech.

Self-downing leads to a barrage of unending self-criticism. Your self-talk is full of nasty comments about yourself: "I am worthless," "I'm insignificant and unimportant," "I'm defective," and "I'm inferior."

Self-downing also interferes with your relationships and goals. Because you see yourself as inferior, you don't assert yourself, even when your rights are being trampled on. You try to make up for what you see as your inadequacy by continually sucking up to others; you go along with what others want and put your own wants and desires on the backburner.

Because you regard yourself as defective, you wrongly assume that you are incapable of carrying out many tasks. You approach your goals expecting to fail, and so attack them only half-heartedly or not at all. You tend to procrastinate or completely avoid working towards the things you want in life.

Finally, and most crucially, your self-downing increases your anxiety causing you to stutter more frequently and more severely while increasing the likelihood of secondary stuttering behaviors such as blinking and rocking, etc.

## Is self-esteem the answer?

Many people who recognize the harmful effect of self-downing recommend developing high self-esteem. We, respectfully, disagree with this recommendation. Here's why.

In order to have high self-esteem, you must see yourself as (1) outstandingly competent and achieving in one or more areas of your life, and/or (2) respected, well-liked, and loved. Perhaps you can achieve these goals much of the time. But being human, and therefore fallible, there will be many times in your life when you fail to reach these goals. What happens to your self-esteem on those occasions?

Maintaining high self-esteem requires eternal vigilance. If you are to retain your high self-esteem, you will need to be unfailingly on your guard against failure and disapproval. Your successes and your charming behavior must be repeated and ongoing.

By striving to develop and maintain self-esteem, you will become perfectionistic, never sure if you have done enough to consider yourself successful or to have earned the respect and admiration of others.

Another danger of high self-esteem is the possibility of going overboard and grandiosely rating yourself as better than everyone else.

When you have high self-esteem, you assume that you will always do well and that others will always approve of you and admire you. You also expect, because you are so deserving, that life will be kind and fair to you. In short, you have inflated expectations for yourself, others, and life in general.

## Introducing unconditional self-acceptance

Unconditional self-acceptance is the 24/7 solution to self-downing. USA requires no self-improvement. You don't have to change a thing except your attitude. USA is available to you no matter what, even when you behave poorly or foolishly, and no matter how severely you stutter. You simply choose to accept yourself — nothing else is required.

## Acceptance is not what you think

When you accept yourself, you don't necessarily like all aspects of yourself. You may, in fact, highly dislike the fact that you stutter or that you have failed to live up to your expectations.

Accepting yourself does not mean that you pretend that you don't care about your speech or any other limitations you have.

You can accept your stuttering while taking steps to increase your fluency. Acceptance does not mean giving up or assuming that you can't change.

## Begin by accepting your stuttering

You may find that accepting yourself is difficult to accomplish at first. You may find it easier to begin by learning to accept the fact that you stutter.

Stuttering is a reality. It won't go away merely because you want it to or because you refuse to acknowledge it. To accept your stuttering, you begin by acknowledging that it is what it is — it exists.

The next step is to recognize that it couldn't be any other way. Given all the known — and unknown — causes of stuttering, and given your genetic, environmental, and psychological history, you have no choice in the matter — you must stutter. Unless you have the power to rewrite your history, you cannot change the fact that you presently stutter, although with work and practice, now and in the future, you might be able to reduce the severity and frequency of your stuttering.

The third step is to acknowledge that you don't have to speak fluently. Fluent speech is not compulsory. You have the right to stutter. You can give yourself permission to speak disfluently.

The fourth step to accept your stuttering is to recognize that stuttering is not completely bad. Although you may not like your stuttering, others may find it endearing. At times, you may get special treatment simply because you stutter. In other words, even the dark cloud of stuttering sometimes has a silver lining.

The fifth step is to acknowledge that stuttering is not fatal. You can stand stuttering — it won't kill you. Whenever you stutter, you don't place yourself in any physical danger. Although you are disfluent, you have the ability to enjoy a full and rich life.

Stuttering is not the end of the world. The sixth step is to see that there are many worse things in life than stuttering. You could, for example, be completely mute, unable to communicate a single word.

Your stuttering does not prevent you from being happy. Even though you stutter, there are many things you can do in life that you will thoroughly enjoy. Stuttering does not prevent you from pursuing your goals. The seventh step is to appreciate all that you can do despite stuttering.

The final step is optional. You can, if you wish, work to improve your fluency. You can accept your stuttering whether or not you work to be more fluent.

## How to accept yourself

You are a complex human being. There are many aspects to you. Stuttering is not the be all and end all of your existence.

Although there are aspects of you that you may not like, including stuttering, no single aspect makes up your entirety. You can choose to like or dislike your stuttering.

Having decided to rate some of your behaviors and difficulties, you begin to accept yourself by acknowledging that an entire human being — including yourself — is unrateable. Humans are far too complex to be given a single, global rating.

Being human, you are imperfect. Everyone is. There's nothing we can do about it, we all have our faults and our flaws. You can work at self-improvement until the cows come home, but you will never be perfect.

Despite your stuttering, you are no more and no less important or worthy than anyone else. Human worth is not measurable. There's no way to measure who is a better human being; there's no way to measure who is more worthy or important. We're all here for the same purpose — whatever that may be, if indeed we have a purpose — and there is no reason to suppose that anyone of us is more (or less) important than the rest.

When you accept yourself, you acknowledge that you don't have to change. You don't have to try to improve yourself or increase your fluency; there is no reason why you must speak fluently.

## Bonus

When you learn to accept your stuttering and to accept yourself, you can extend this to everyone else on the planet. You can accept everyone no matter how badly they treat you or how badly they behave. When you learn to accept others, you will no longer feel angry or envious. You will become a more compassionate, dignified human being.

**Remember this:**

- Self-acceptance is the best alternative to self-downing.

- Self-acceptance can lead to greater fluency.

# 9 SPEECH MANIPULATION

**In this chapter you will:**

- Develop your REBT skills in tandem with new speech manipulation techniques.

- Learn how to directly control your stuttering.

To move from stuttering to fluency involves two steps: (1) managing your emotions and (2) directly manipulating your speech. The bulk of this book is devoted to the first step — managing your emotions.

This chapter provides you with the second piece of the puzzle. Here you'll learn how to directly manipulate your speech so you can overcome your stuttering. It's important that you continue to practice REBT while manipulating your speech. The better you are at managing your emotions, the easier you'll find it to manipulate your speech. Conversely, the more time you dedicate to practicing speech manipulation, the easier you will find it to manage your emotions.

You may be reluctant to try some of the exercises in this

chapter, possibly because of a fear of failure or a fear of looking foolish. We encourage you to use REBT to overcome your fears and your reluctance. Remember: your fears and reluctance are caused by irrational beliefs. If you use REBT to get rid of your irrational beliefs, you'll get rid of your fears and reluctance.

## Voluntary pseudo-stuttering

Voluntary pseudo-stuttering (sometimes called *deliberate disfluency*) is a powerful technique you can use to greatly reduce your stuttering-related anxiety, to get used to stuttering in public, and to gain greater control over your speech while at the same time learning not to feel ashamed or embarrassed about stuttering. The technique has three parts to it: (1) encouraging yourself with silent self-talk; (2) deliberately stuttering; and (3) learning an easier way to stutter by "bouncing" the sounds that make up words.

## The benefits of voluntary pseudo-stuttering bouncing exercises

Voluntary pseudo-stuttering, along with the other exercises you'll learn, desensitize you, that is, they eliminate your fear of stuttering. At the same time, they teach you how to control your anxiety so that you are able to reduce the frequency and severity of your stuttering. The more you practice voluntary pseudo-stuttering, the more control you will have over your emotions. With greater control over your emotions you'll be able to better manage your stuttering. Additionally, you'll be able to prove to yourself that nothing terrible happens when you stutter. You'll see that nobody dies, nobody faints, nobody vomits, and nobody calls the cops. There is literally nothing to be afraid of.

Over the years, your mind has come to associate

speaking with fear; the emotional control center in your brain (called the *amygdala*) has learned to produce fear each time you speak. With voluntary pseudo-stuttering, you will retrain your amygdala to ignore your stuttering so you can speak — and stutter — without fear. When you speak without fear, you'll find it much easier to manage your fluency and eventually attain spontaneous fluency in public — the same fluency you have when you are alone, talking to yourself.

To feel confident using voluntary pseudo-stuttering, you can practice it in private, on your own, or with the help of a therapist or trusted friend or family member before practicing it in public. When you do these exercises in the sequence specified, you'll develop a sense of control over your speech and your body.

## How to master voluntary pseudo-stuttering

To get started using voluntary pseudo-stuttering, select a word you would not normally have trouble saying. Before saying the word, give yourself some encouragement. Silently tell yourself, "I can do this. Nothing bad will happen."

While standing in front of a mirror or while facing a partner, say the word out loud making sure that you repeat the first sound. For example, suppose the word you have selected to work with is the word "president." Say, "p- p- p- p- p- president." (Picture a basketballer bouncing the ball a few times to find his rhythm and steady himself before shooting for the basket. When you deliberately repeat the first sound, it's as though you are "bouncing" the sound before you "shoot" from the final repetition of the sound into saying the word "president.")

After you have practiced pseudo-voluntary stuttering on words you usually do not stutter on, you'll be able to practice the technique with words you have difficulty saying. Practicing voluntary pseudo-stuttering on words you have difficulty with is particularly useful if you have a severe stutter. With these troublesome words, deliberately increase the severity or duration of your stutter. If you normally repeat the first sound, for example five times, deliberately repeat (bounce) the sound an extra five or six times before completing (shooting for) the word. This is a most important step in overcoming unhealthy emotions and unhelpful beliefs about your stuttering.

As you are repeating the first sound of the word out loud, continue giving yourself silent encouragement. Tell yourself, "This is okay. Even though I don't like stuttering I can handle it". After you've said the full word, give yourself further encouragement, "I did it. It was fine. No problems. I felt a little uncomfortable initiating the stuttering and prolonging it, but I could stand the discomfort."

Once you feel confident using this technique with a single word, practice with two words in a row. Deliberately stutter on each of the words. Again, make sure you give yourself silent encouragement before, during, and after saying each of the words.

Practice this technique at home for 10 minutes each morning and for five minutes each evening. You can also practice voluntary pseudo-stuttering any other time you're alone, such as when you're in your car or in the shower.

As soon as possible, start using the technique in public while talking to people you know or while speaking to strangers. For example, you can practice while talking to the clerk at the checkout counter. Be sure to give yourself plenty of encouragement with silent self-talk whenever you use this technique in public. It's normal to feel some tension before you practice voluntary pseudo-stuttering in public. But the tension you feel won't kill you. You can stand it, especially if you tell yourself forcefully and repeatedly that you can stand it. After a while, the tension will disappear and you'll be able to pseudo-stutter without any anxiety.

To get the most from voluntary pseudo-stuttering, use it in combination with the following exercises while motivating yourself with encouraging self-talk.

## Eliminating secondary stuttering symptoms

Secondary symptoms are the things you do along with stuttering such as snapping your fingers or blinking your eyes. They also include such things as avoidances and substitution. With the help of another person, write down all of your secondary stuttering symptoms. One by one, take each symptom and exaggerate the duration, severity, and frequency of the symptom. Practice until you can start and stop each symptom whenever you want. In time, you'll be able to take control of the secondary symptoms and prevent them from happening in the first place.

Don't expect instant success with this technique. It will take time. Don't forget to use REBT to overcome any anxiety while you're practicing this technique.

## Cancellation

A good time to practice voluntary pseudo-stuttering is after you have stumbled on a word. You may have had a block — with or without sound — or you may have stuttered the word. Once you have eventually said the word, pause for approximately 2 to 5 seconds, then repeat the word, deliberately stuttering by using easy, bounce repetitions.

## Bounce your way out of disfluency

When you get stuck on a word, whether through repetition or a block, stick with it. Remain in the same mode (repetition or block) until you feel confident you can get out of it. But instead of getting out of it the way you usually do, gradually ease your way out of the repetition or block with easy, bouncing repetitions.

## Pre-emption of oncoming stutters

Whenever you hear the footsteps of an oncoming block or repetition, instead of trying to say the word as you usually do, pre-empt the block or involuntary repetition with an easy, deliberate, bouncing repetition.

## Making progress with voluntary pseudo-stuttering

Once you have mastered voluntary pseudo-stuttering in public, you can practice taking control of your speech. Whenever you have an involuntary stutter, make a deliberate switch to voluntary pseudo-stuttering. Voluntary stuttering is much less severe and gives you greater control over your speech.

By choosing to stutter with voluntary pseudo-stuttering and bouncing into your words, you put yourself in the driver's seat and can easily reduce the frequency and severity of involuntary stuttering until you can eventually avoid it altogether. In time, most people won't notice that you stutter.

How well does this technique work? In order to complete my Doctorate of Psychology, I (G.N.) worked as an intern with Cancer Lifeline in Seattle. My duties included answering and talking on the phone for six to eight hours each day! During the entire year there were no complaints about my speaking. None. Not once did I feel out of control. Nor did I have a severe block. I was able to maintain this level of fluency by using voluntary pseudo-stuttering every now and again to remind my amygdala that stuttering and panic do not have to go hand-in-hand.

But don't take our word for it. Try voluntary pseudo-stuttering. Teach your amygdala that there is nothing terrible, awful, or horrible about stuttering. And in the meantime, you will have taught yourself that if you do have an involuntary stutter, it's not the end of the world and that stuttering does not make you less of a human being.

In addition to voluntary pseudo-stuttering, here are some other techniques you can use to directly manipulate your speech.

## Elongation of vowels

As you talk, deliberately elongate your vowels wherever they occur in the word. Many people who stutter find that this elongation of vowels helps to relieve the pressure we put on ourselves to speak fluently. Don't forget, you can also relieve the pressure on yourself by using encouraging self-talk.

## Easy onsets

At the start of a phrase or sentence, breathe out softly, allowing air to pass silently over your vocal folds. As the air evaporates, gently introduce the first sound of the phrase or sentence. This is an easy way to begin a sentence that may pre-empt any stuttering. Use REBT and encouraging self-talk to remain calm as you practice this technique.

## Conclusion

REBT and the exercises described in this chapter take practice. The more you practice, especially when you practice accepting your stuttering and accepting yourself, the easier the exercises will become, and the more you will get out of them.

Remember, the goal of these exercises is not to help you hide your stuttering — which is counter-productive; the goal is to help you move forward in your speech. Keep using these exercises even as your speech improves. Continued practice of these exercises will help you to prevent a relapse.

**Remember this:**

- Use speech manipulation techniques in tandem with REBT.

- The more you practice voluntary pseudo-stuttering, the easier it gets and the faster you'll make progress.

# 10 THE PAYOFF

---

**In this chapter you will:**

- Develop a helpful attitude towards stuttering.

- Put new skills into practice and reap the rewards

- Learn that persistence will bring you rewards.

---

## How to Think More Clearly about Stuttering

This book has a very clear and simple message: when you accept the fact that you stutter and accept yourself despite your stuttering, you will feel less anxious and ashamed, and will probably stutter less severely and less frequently. If you add the speech manipulation techniques you learned in chapter 9, then you'll make great strides of progress with respect to the frequency and severity of stuttering.

The number one ingredient of acceptance is a flexible, non-demanding attitude towards yourself and towards stuttering. The minute you convince — yes, convince — yourself that you don't have to speak fluently, you will have taken a giant leap towards accepting your stuttering and accepting yourself. Conversely, the more you insist on speaking perfectly fluently, the more anxious and ashamed you'll feel, and the more severely and frequently you'll stutter.

The mere idea of accepting your stuttering, of not demanding or insisting on fluency, may seem counterintuitive. For years, you've been telling yourself you must not stutter and must speak fluently. Now, we're advising you to tell yourself the opposite: you don't have to speak fluently and you are allowed to stutter. Paradoxically, the less you resist stuttering, the more fluently you'll speak. And the less you beat yourself up, the less anxious and ashamed you'll feel.

Giving yourself permission to stutter is the first step towards a life of freedom — freedom from shame and anxiety and greater freedom from stuttering. But it's only the first step. It takes commitment and effort to accept yourself and your stuttering. In order to benefit from acceptance, you must practice it daily for the rest of your life. Acceptance is not a "set it and forget it" phenomenon. It's a habit, like brushing your teeth or showering. Just as you practice personal hygiene every day, you must also practice mental hygiene every day.

The best way to practice acceptance is to do it! But if you're like most people, you may not know how to begin. Fortunately, Albert Ellis, the creator of Rational Emotive Behavior Therapy on which this book is based, and his colleagues have formulated a variety of exercises to help you develop your ability to accept the fact that you stutter and accept yourself despite your stuttering. You can experiment with these exercises to see which ones work best for you.

It's vitally important that you actually do these exercises.

Don't expect any value from merely reading them. If you read them without putting them into action, you are wasting your time and will do nothing to overcome your stuttering, your shame, and your anxiety. If you don't intend to do the exercises, you may as well stop reading now. In fact, you may as well give this book to a friend and forget you ever read it. Reading this book will not help you. Success and mastery come from doing the exercises. Do them!

Some of the exercises require you to do nothing more than think — really think! — about some ideas that may be new to you. Others will help you to change your emotions when they interfere with your goals. The rest of the exercises will help you to put your new thinking and feeling skills into action so that you can approach any speaking occasion with confidence.

Of course, we don't want you to neglect the physical side of stuttering: the forcing and the struggling. Keep using the techniques you learned in the last chapter to whittle away at the struggling, forcing, and avoiding. Keep it simple. You'll probably find that just introducing easy bouncing re-re-repetitions once in a while will do the trick. Or you may have to learn to use these e-e-easy repetitions whenever you hear the sound of an oncoming stutter or find yourself struggling with a block.

But back to thinking. You can use a number of REBT thinking exercises to make it easier for you to accept the fact that you stutter and accept yourself despite your stuttering. At first, some of these ideas may seem strange, but as you rehearse them and take time to consider them you'll begin to see that they make far more sense than much of the nonsense you've been telling yourself for years.

Very few people pause to think about their thoughts and

beliefs. As a result, they often think in ways that are unhelpful and hold beliefs that are untrue. If you take the time to think about your beliefs and to question them, you may be surprised to see how many of them are untrue, illogical, and unhelpful. Specifically, you can ask yourself three questions:

1. Does it help me over the long run to believe this?

2. Is this idea consistent with the facts? And

3. Does the idea make logical sense?

For example, take the idea that you must not stutter and ask yourself the three questions. Does it help you over the long run to believe this? No, it doesn't help you. It makes you anxious and depressed. Is the idea consistent with the facts? No, there is no law of the universe that says you must not stutter. Does the idea make logical sense? No. It does not follow logically that just because you want to speak without stuttering that you must not stutter.

Once you've answered these three questions, you can formulate a statement of fact that helps you cope with stuttering. For example, "I want to speak fluently but there is no reason why I must be fluent" or "I don't like it when I stutter, but I can live happily and successfully no matter how much I stutter." Write down the statement so that you can refer to it regularly. Carry the statement around with you at all times. Whenever you feel yourself becoming anxious at the thought of speaking, take out the statement and read it to yourself, thinking carefully about its implications. And remember all the time you are taking out the struggle and forcing, the avoidances and pauses out of your speech. Your speech is becoming easier and more forward moving.

You can also make recordings of yourself reciting these

rational, coping statements. You can put these recordings on your iPod or similar device and play them to yourself over and over.

You might have trouble convincing yourself that you don't have to speak perfectly. If so, make a list of the advantages and disadvantages of believing that you must not stutter. If you make an honest effort in compiling the list, you'll see that there are a few advantages to believing that you must speak fluently and many disadvantages. Read over the list often until you convince yourself that insisting on perfect fluency does not help you.

At times, you may feel that stuttering is the worst possible thing that could happen to a human being. However, disfluency is not the worst thing that can happen. Remind yourself that stuttering is not the end of the world. In fact, you can learn from it. You can see that you have survived whenever you've stuttered in the past. With this kind of self-awareness, you can approach every speaking opportunity knowing that you'll get through it.

Get into the habit of thinking rationally about speaking (and about life in general). To help yourself in this regard, read books by Albert Ellis including, *A Guide to Rational Living* and *How to Stubbornly Refuse to Make Yourself Miserable About Anything — Yes, Anything.*

Teach REBT philosophy and practice to your friends and family. Teaching these ideas will not only make you more aware of them, but will also help you to make them an integral part of your belief system. In other words, you'll be helping your friends and family as well as helping yourself.

Follow the example of other people who have not let their stuttering hold them back, including Tiger Woods, James Earl Jones, and Bruce Willis. How do they respond under difficult conditions? If you model yourself on these famous (and not so famous) stutterers, your own confidence will rise. By following their example as they calmly deal with their stuttering, you can imitate their behavior and deal with your stuttering in a sensible, calm manner.

## How to Feel Better about Stuttering

You can use a number of REBT feeling exercises to accept the fact that you stutter and accept yourself despite your stuttering. These exercises will help you to feel better — without fear, shame, or embarrassment — when you stutter.

Begin by adding emotion to your coping statements. Take the rational coping statements you created earlier and make them stronger. For example "I want to speak fluently but there is absolutely no reason why I must stop stuttering. None! None! None!" or "If I stutter badly that's just too damned bad!" or "By manipulating my attitudes and my speech, my speech is getting more flowing, more forward moving." Say these to yourself with great feeling, emphasizing each word as you say it. The more force and energy you put into these statements, the more effective it will be in helping you to cope with stuttering.

You can use your imagination to overcome the shame and anxiety that go along with stuttering. Imagine yourself stuttering while talking to someone you want to impress. Allow yourself to feel anxious. Really feel it. With the image of stuttering still in your mind, change your feelings to concern and optimism. How? By changing the fear-creating, irrational thoughts into rational thoughts, or by remembering your rational coping statements. Make sure that you don't change the image (for example, don't see yourself speaking fluently). Practice this technique (called "rational emotive imagery") for a few minutes every day until you are able to spontaneously feel calm whenever you are about to speak.

Shame and anxiety are often associated with the fear of looking foolish. One of the most effective ways of overcoming the fear of looking foolish is to deliberately do foolish things in front of others and to see for yourself that nothing bad really happens. Instead of trying to act "cool," practice doing silly things in public. For example, tell someone you were just released from a mental hospital and ask them what day of the week it is. Your goal is to do these "shameful" acts without feeling ashamed or embarrassed, and to realize that you don't need others' approval. Don't do anything that will get you arrested or fired from your job. Also be careful not to do anything that will hurt others. But in order to change you have to be aware of your feelings and thoughts.

You can use humor to overcome your fear of speaking in public. One humorous technique you can use is to imagine a situation where you stutter in public and exaggerate what happens as a result of your stuttering. For example you could imagine a headline on the front page of a national newspaper telling the world how you stuttered during a job interview. Picture everyone you know avoiding you because you stutter. In reality, it's likely that nothing this bad will ever happen to you. But if you can face a situation as daunting as this while retaining your sense of humor, nothing will faze you. Be creative and have fun with this exercise.

Frequently remind yourself of the basics of unconditional self-acceptance. Unconditional self-acceptance is a process, a series of steps you follow in order to accept yourself no matter what. This process involves the following steps:

- Acknowledging that you would rather speak fluently than stutter

- Recognizing that you will sometimes stutter

- Admitting that you can sometimes improve your fluency with effort, and sometimes not improve, no matter what you do

- Understanding that you control your feelings by controlling your thoughts

- Realizing that it's not the end of the world to stutter

- Knowing that stuttering is not fatal

- Strongly believing that there is no reason why you absolutely must speak fluently

- Being aware that given your makeup (including your genes, your upbringing, your experiences, and your self-talk), it makes sense that you will stutter from time to time — that is the way it should be

- Convincing yourself that stuttering does not make you a failed human being

- Deciding that whether you speak fluently or stutter, you will make it your goal to enjoy life

## Behavioral exercises to boost confidence

REBT has a range of highly effective activities you can use to accept the fact that you stutter and accept yourself despite your stuttering.

Just do it! Throw yourself into speaking opportunities with enthusiasm. Even if you don't feel confident, act as though you do. Acting in ways that contradict your fears by doing what you are afraid of will show you that nothing terrible happens when you speak, even if you stutter severely. In particular, seek out opportunities to do what you fear. If you're afraid of job interviews, apply for as many different jobs as you can. Keep working at it until you no longer fear interviews. If you dislike talking on the telephone because of your stuttering, start making phone calls just for the practice. For example, call the local cinema and ask about screening times, even if you have no desire to see the movie you're enquiring about. Remember using deliberate disfluencies, also known as voluntary stuttering is very helpful.

Reward yourself whenever you work to overcome your fear of speaking, and penalize yourself whenever you deliberately avoid facing up to it. Rewarding yourself when you speak and penalizing yourself when you avoid speaking can act as a quick and powerful method to boost your confidence in speaking situations.

From time to time, deliberately stutter. When you stutter deliberately, you'll notice that there is nothing to be ashamed of and nothing to fear. You'll see that stuttering is not fatal. The more often you stutter deliberately, without shame or fear, the less shame and fear you'll experience when your stuttering is involuntary.

## The power of persistence

These REBT exercises are designed to help you overcome shame and anxiety, two of the most common emotions associated with stuttering. Overcoming shame and anxiety is reward enough, but as a bonus, especially if you play around with easy bounces, you may also discover that you stutter less frequently and less severely. This makes these exercises well worth your time and effort.

Treat each of these exercises as an experiment to see how well they work for you. You will probably need to test each one numerous times to get the most benefit from them. Don't judge yourself by how well the exercises work for you. If you find, after using one of these exercises for a time that it doesn't help you much, try another one. Keep working at it.

## A final word

Look for ways to make life more enjoyable. Learn to think of communicating with others as a rewarding experience, not as a chance to prove your worth. Never forget that there is more to life than speaking fluently. It's possible that you may never become a totally fluent speaker. However, that is no reason not to make the most of your life. In fact, enjoying yourself is the best revenge; it's a way of saying to the universe, "You may have made life more difficult for me by making me a person who stutters, but I'm not going to allow that to hold me back. In fact, I'm going to be even more determined to see that I squeeze every ounce of enjoyment out of life that I possible can!"

**Remember this:**

- Changing the way you think about yourself and about stuttering has a powerful effect on your feelings.

- Practice is the key to self-acceptance and fluency.

- For the time being, at this instant, accept that you stutter the way you stutter and still can have a wonderful time on this earth.

- As you practice the techniques described in this book your emotions about speaking—anxiety, guilt, shame, and low tolerance of frustration will dissolve.

- Your self-downing will turn into unconditional self-acceptance.

- You might still have some stutters but they will be much less frequent and exhibit less forcing and struggling.

- You will be as fluent or almost as fluent as when you talk to yourself alone.

- You will feel as much at ease talking to people as when you talk alone.

- You may gain spontaneous fluency: no struggle, no forcing, no emotional upsets, no desire to avoid, and no desire to stop talking.

- You'll easily handle remaining stuttering or short lapses because you'll know that you're in charge.

- You will not let the remnants of your stuttering interfere with your life.

- Should — in the very unlikely event — our system not work for you or should you decide that upon doing a cost/benefit analysis what we ask will cost you more in expenditure in time, energy and money, you can still have unconditional self-acceptance with or without stuttering by simply choosing it.

- Stuttering cannot, and does not have to, define you; you have thousands of other characteristics and roles to let yourself be defined by the one aspect of that you don't like.

- Stuttering cannot, and does not, make you a less worthwhile person. It cannot — in the terms of street language — make you a child of a lesser god. You can still make life a moveable feast.

# APPENDIX

# A DOZEN OF THE BEST

This is the first book ever published that shows you how to apply rational emotive behavior therapy (REBT) to stuttering. But there are dozens, perhaps hundreds, of other REBT books available (Albert Ellis, the original creator of REBT, wrote over 80 books on the subject). In book stores and in your local library, you can find REBT books that will show you — among other things — how to improve your relationships, how to lose weight, how to overcome procrastination, and how to manage your money better.

In this section, we have selected 12 of the best books that we think will be of interest to you as you learn to apply REBT to stuttering. We believe this is the cream of the REBT crop.

*A Guide to Rational Living* by Albert Ellis and Robert A. Harper. This is perhaps the most important self-help book ever published. Written by the creators of REBT and now in its third edition, this book has sold over 1.5 million copies worldwide. The authors take a no-nonsense approach and show how we create our own emotions and what we can do to feel better and deal with our problems more effectively. They discuss 10 common, irrational ideas that interfere with our happiness, creativity, and productivity and show us how to break free from these crippling ideas.

*A Rational Counseling Primer* by Howard S. Young. This is a very brief introduction to rational emotive behavior therapy and is ideal for teenagers. This booklet is very easy to read with amusing diagrams to reinforce the author's points. Howard Young shows you how it's much easier to make yourself happy if you do not exaggerate your problems and demand that things be different from the way they really are.

*Choose to Be Happy* by Wayne Froggatt. This book will show you a step-by-step method to become your own therapist. Some of the finer points of rational emotive behavior therapy can be complex and subtle. In this book, the author explains those concepts in a language and style that is very easy to follow. In Part One, he explains the theory and practice of REBT. In the second part, he shows you how to apply the theory and practice to common problems. As well as anger, anxiety, and depression, he shows you how you can use REBT to become more assertive, more decisive, and self-motivated.

*Fearless* by Wayne Froggatt. There are many types of anxiety: worry, panic attacks, avoidance behavior, social anxiety, obsessions and compulsions, health anxiety, phobias, and post-traumatic anxiety, to name a few. In this book, you'll learn the causes of anxiety. You'll learn how to assess your own anxiety and develop a plan to overcome it. You'll learn a range of techniques that you can apply to help you overcome your particular form of anxiety. As a bonus, you'll learn some strategies that will help you to relax, to sleep better, and to solve your day-to-day problems.

*Feeling Better, Getting Better, Staying Better* by Albert Ellis. There are many things you can do to feel better so you no longer feel angry, anxious, or depressed. But feeling better is not enough. Getting better is much more important. When you get better, you'll not only feel better, you'll continue to feel better for long periods of time, you'll spend more time doing things you want to do, you'll rarely make yourself upset, and you'll know what to do on those rare occasions when you do make yourself upset. In this book, Albert Ellis explains some of the techniques that will help you to feel better and, more importantly, he shows you how to use rational emotive behavior therapy to get better and to stay better.

*Hold Your Head up High* by Paul Hauck. Dr Hauck is one of REBT's most popular writers. In this book, he shows you how to forget about judging yourself, and how to get on with your life without the feelings of shame, failure, embarrassment, and anxiety that are holding you back. You'll learn how to accept yourself as you are, warts and all, without relying on other people's opinions. This book shows how your sense of inferiority is not based on what you do or how you do it; it's based on what you tell yourself. By changing the script in your head you can become calm, confident, and assertive, no matter what happens to you.

*How to Control Your Anxiety before It Controls You* by Albert Ellis. Some anxiety — when it is healthy and based on feelings of concern, caution, and vigilance — is good for you because it discourages you from taking life-threatening risks. But unhealthy anxiety can paralyze you and prevent you from enjoying everyday activities and relationships; it causes you to make mistakes and to underperform. In this book, Albert Ellis shows that you can control your anxiety and enjoy more success, pleasure, and happiness once you realize that things and people do not make you anxious. You create your own anxiety with unrealistic expectations and by making mountains out of mole hills. Dr Ellis opens up his casebook to show how his clients have used REBT to overcome their anxiety, and how you can use it to overcome yours.

*How to Stubbornly Refuse to Make Yourself Miserable about Anything — Yes, Anything!* by Albert Ellis. Dr Ellis shows us how we can teach ourselves to overcome our problems without getting unnecessarily upset or miserable. He argues that emotions such as anger, anxiety, and depression are not only unnecessary, they are unethical. When we make ourselves upset, we add to the sum of human misery by being unfair and unjust to ourselves. Because we choose to think the thoughts that make us upset, we can just as easily choose to think alternative thoughts and stubbornly refuse to make ourselves miserable.

*Stage Fright: 40 Stars Tell You How They Beat America's #1 Fear* by Mick Berry and Michael R. Edelstein. As well as showing how to use REBT to overcome the fear of talking to others, the authors interview 40 of the most highly-accomplished public figures including Melissa Etheridge, Robin Williams, Jason Alexander, Mose Allison, Maya Angelou, David Brenner, Peter Coyote, Olympia Dukakis, Phyllis Diller, Richard Lewis. The stars offer tips on dealing with fear of performing and fear of public speaking.

*Overcoming Worry and Fear* by Paul Hauck. Anxiety is a much more common problem than anger or depression; and when it strikes, it tends to persist longer than the other two unhealthy emotions. For many people, it is a lifelong companion. The author argues that we have been trained to believe worrying thoughts, and this training takes over whenever we face stressful conditions. He shows how worry is a habit, and like all habits, it can be broken. In this book, you'll learn some simple techniques you can use to relax, take your problems in stride, and reach your full potential.

*Three Minute Therapy* by Michael R. Edelstein and David Ramsay Steele. In this jargon-free book, the authors show how you can change your life by changing your thinking. Throughout the book, they show you how you can apply the main theories and practices of REBT to overcome your problems using a technique that takes only three minutes to complete. By using the three-minute exercise, you'll find that your emotional troubles seem less mysterious and have less control over you, and you'll be able to effectively and efficiently reduce or eliminate some of your worst fears and anxieties.

*SOS Help for Emotions* by Lynn Clark. Albert Ellis called this book "a gem of an introduction to REBT." This book will help you to manage anxiety, anger, depression, and other unpleasant feelings. The author provides numerous ideas and activities that can help you to attain greater contentment and reach your personal goals. You'll learn how to effectively handle life's problems and frustrations and better manage your relationships with others. If you'd like to increase your self-knowledge and have greater control over your unpleasant emotions, then this book is for you.

These are some of the best self-help books on the market. We strongly encourage you to read at least one of them. See if your local library carries any of them. If not, ask your librarian to order them for your library, or ask about an interlibrary loan.

# THOUGHT MANAGEMENT

Do you spend a lot of time thinking about stuttering? Many people who stutter spend countless hours haunted by upsetting thoughts; they dwell on persistent — often unwanted — ideas and images that trigger emotional distress. If you find you have become preoccupied, or totally absorbed, with stuttering, you will benefit from learning how to manage your thoughts.

Thought management is a technique that lets you decide when you will think about stuttering, how long you will think about it and, most importantly, when you won't think about it. The technique has three steps:

1. Focusing on a particular thought for a specified period of time.

2. Shifting your focus away from the thought to another idea. And

3. Restricting the times you think about stuttering to specific times of the day.

## The benefits of thought management

Thought management is a powerful technique that allows

you to have peace of mind. It teaches you to control your thinking and free up your mind so you can think of more things other than stuttering — things that are either more pleasant, lead to solving other problems you face, or thoughts that are creative and fulfilling. By getting rid of unwanted thoughts and images, thought management eradicates the unpleasant emotions you feel as a result of your obsessive thoughts. Once you gain control of your thoughts, you'll feel more confident in social situations because you won't be plagued by unpleasant images of failure and rejection.

If unwanted thoughts keep you awake at night, learning to control those thoughts and turn them off will help you to get a better night's sleep. During the day, instead of dwelling on your speech and planning ways to avoid social situations, you'll spend your time planning and doing all the exciting things you've ever wanted to do.

## How to master thought management

To get started with thought management, you will need to set aside a lengthy period of time — perhaps as much as two or three hours — where you can be by yourself without interruption. Turn off the television, your iPod, and your cellphone. Make yourself comfortable and intentionally think about an unpleasant thought or image that you are often troubled by, such as stuttering in public. Hold on to that thought, and keep it in mind for as long as you can. If other thoughts intrude and you find yourself thinking about something else — as is most likely to happen — gently shift the focus back to the unpleasant thought. Continue dwelling on the unpleasant thought or image until you grow bored with it or until it no longer upsets you.

You may think that intentionally focusing on a single

thought or image — without interruption — for several hours is a waste of time. But compare it to how much time you already spend dwelling on the unpleasant thought. After you have forced yourself to focus on the unpleasant thought for several hours, you'll have no desire to think about it any longer. In future, when the thought or image intrudes, you will have had your fill of it, and will no longer entertain it.

At this point, a simple warning is called for. Thinking about an unpleasant event for several hours will cause your blood pressure to rise. Therefore, if you already have problems with high blood pressure, we advise you not to attempt this technique and move directly on to the second phase.

The second phase of thought management involves focusing on an unwanted thought for a much shorter period of time. Before you begin this phase, make a list of unwanted thoughts that you find difficult to get rid of. Make a second list of pleasant thoughts, ideas, and images you enjoy thinking about. Choose one item from each list — one unpleasant thought and one pleasant thought. Once again, make yourself comfortable and focus on the unpleasant thought or image. Hold onto that thought for a minute or so then yell out, "Stop!" As soon as you say "stop," switch your focus to the pleasant thought.

Practice switching your thoughts several times per day. Whenever you have a few minutes to yourself, focus on the unpleasant thought before suddenly interrupting it by yelling out, "Stop," and switching your focus to the same pleasant thought. Continue practicing this technique until you have no trouble interrupting an unpleasant thought and replacing it with a more pleasant alternative.

In the final phase of thought management, you set aside specific times of the day — for example, 10 a.m., 1 p.m., and 7:30 p.m. — to focus on the unpleasant thought. At these times, you spend only two or three minutes dwelling on the thought. After entertaining the thought for a short while, you forget about it and get on with your day. If you notice the thought intruding on you at other times of the day, use the thought switching method and remind yourself that you will have an opportunity to dwell on the thought at the next appointed time.

## Advanced thought management

After you have mastered thought management when you're on your own, it's time to practice it in public, especially in difficult situations. If you notice that unpleasant thoughts pop into your head whenever you're about to speak to someone, shout "Stop!" And switch your focus to the more pleasant thought. In public, when you shout "Stop," you might want to do so silently, in your mind. If the silent "Stop" isn't as effective as you would like in helping to shift your focus to the more pleasant thought, you can slap yourself on the wrist or the back of your hand to distract your attention away from the unpleasant thought. Alternatively, you can wear a rubber band around your wrist and snap the rubber band so it hurts. The mild, temporary pain of the rubber band snapping against your wrist will distract you and remind you to focus on more pleasant images or ideas.

Eliminating unwanted thoughts when you're in public will dramatically decrease your anxiety. You'll feel far more relaxed talking to others and may find — as a bonus — that was practice, as you grow more proficient at thought management, you become substantially more fluent. The only way to find out is to try it.

# RATIONAL EMOTIVE IMAGERY

By now, you've probably grasped the main ideas of rational emotive behavior therapy (REBT): You know that you create your feelings with your thoughts and beliefs; you know that many of your feelings are unhelpful; and you know that, with work and practice, you can change your unhelpful feelings into more helpful emotions by changing your thoughts and beliefs.

You may have tried to put these concepts into practice. Hopefully, you've seen the benefits of changing your beliefs and have experienced the emotional relief that follows from changing your beliefs.

However, many people who try REBT for the first time report that while they can see that their old, irrational beliefs are, indeed, irrational and the rational alternatives are, in fact, rational, they don't notice any change in their feelings.

If you've had this experience, you may benefit from rational emotive imagery (REI).

Rational emotive imagery is a technique that helps you to practice feeling the way you want to feel in difficult situations. By using your imagination, you see yourself using rational self-talk and coping with difficult situations. By frequently imagining yourself coping with difficult situations, you'll find it much easier to cope with them in real life.

## The benefits of rational emotive imagery

Rational emotive imagery allows you to decide, in advance, how you want to feel in difficult situations. For example, instead of feeling anxious whenever you talk in meetings or contribute to a class discussion, you may want to feel appropriately concerned. (In this context, appropriately concerned means that you want to speak knowledgeably and coherently without stressing over it).

REI provides you with an opportunity to experiment with a variety of rational coping statements and gauge for yourself which ones have the most powerful effect on your feelings.

## How to master rational emotive imagery

Before you begin using REI, you will need to think of a difficult situation and the emotion you want to feel in that situation — the more difficult the situation, the better. For example, you might imagine yourself stuttering in a job interview and the interviewer showing his or her impatience with you.

When you choose the emotion you want to feel in this situation, it's important that you choose a realistic, helpful emotion. For example, it would not be helpful for you to feel angry, nor would be realistic for you to feel indifferent or happy. A realistic, useful emotion in this situation would be to feel disappointed — disappointed with your speech and disappointed with the response of the interviewer.

Once you've chosen a situation and a helpful emotional response, make yourself comfortable by lying on sitting down with your eyes closed and imagine yourself in the situation. Let yourself feel upset — angry, anxious, ashamed, etc. Allow these unhelpful feelings to grow stronger so that you feel them intensely.

Now, without changing your image of the situation in any way, change your feelings so you experience only the emotion you want to feel in the situation. Continue to imagine yourself stuttering and the interviewer showing his or her impatience until you can see it clearly and feel only disappointed.

Once you've changed your emotions and feel only disappointed, ask yourself what you said to yourself to bring about the change. What were the words you used to stop yourself feeling angry, anxious, or ashamed? What words helped you to feel disappointed without feeling overwhelmed?

In all probability you will have brought about the change by thinking about the situation in a rational, self-helping way. For example, you may have told yourself, "I wish I wasn't stuttering so badly and could express myself more fluently. I also wish that the interviewer would show more patience with me. But, if I continue to stutter and he or she continues to be impatient, it's not the end of the world. I don't have to be fluent, and the interviewer doesn't have to be patient."

## Advanced rational emotive imagery

Albert Ellis, the creator of rational emotive behavior therapy, recommends practicing REI at least once a day for 30 days. In time, with frequent practice of REI, you'll find that you automatically respond to difficult situations in a self-helping manner which is calm, courageous, and compassionate.

As you get more experienced using REI, you can

visualize yourself in ever more "gruesome" situations — situations that are far more difficult than you're likely to find in real life. When you can see yourself coping with these extreme situations, you'll have very little difficulty coping with the less extreme, everyday situations you're actually likely to find yourself in.

# CONTACT THE AUTHOR

**Dr. Gunars Neiders:**
Phone – 206-399-4451
Email - Dr.Neiders@gmail.com
Skype - Gunarsneiders
Website – www.stutteringpsychotherapy.com
Facebook – www.Facebook.com/DrNeiders
Twitter – www.Twitter.com/DrNeiders
LinkedIn – www.LinkedIn.com/in/DrNeiders

**Gunars K. Neiders, Ph.D.E.E., Psy.D.** is a licensed psychologist in the State of Washington. Dr. Neiders provides in-person and internet-based (Skype, Google Hangout) psychotherapy. These psychotherapy modalities are augmented by telephone and e-mail contacts. Dr. Neiders **specializes in coaching** — via Skype and Google Hangout — **persons who want to minimize the frequency and severity of their stuttering and lead productive and emotionally fulfilling lives**. The current book: *From Stuttering to Fluency: Manage Your Emotions and Live More Fully* is based on his coaching experience, work done with Albert Ellis (his mentor), as well as on his dissertation: *Theoretical Development Of A Proposed Rational Emotive Behavior Therapy Based Model To Treat Persons With Chronic Perseverative Stuttering Syndrome*, and his study of the Stuttering Modification techniques from speech and language pathologists. His website – www.stutteringpsychotherapy.com – will contain a companion workbook blog. This blog will provide step-by-step practical therapy exercises. The exercises can be used for self-help and in individual and group therapy settings.

He is a member of the American Speech-Language-Hearing Association and is a member of SID4, the Special Interest Group on Fluency and Fluency Disorders. He is a long time member (over 45 years) of the National Stuttering Association, where in the 1970s he was the local leader of the Seattle Chapter.

**Will Ross** tutors REBT self-helpers and is the author and publisher of online REBT self-help materials. He is the webmaster and co-founder of REBTnetwork.org, established in 2006 to promote Rational Emotive Behavior Therapy (REBT) and the life & work of its creator, Dr. Albert Ellis, Ph.D. He is the author of *A Guide to Shameless Happiness* and the co-author of *Rational Drinking: How to Live Happily With or Without Alcohol.*

Made in the USA
San Bernardino, CA
19 October 2016